Sydney Higgins is a writer, educationalist and broadcaster. Born in Cornwall, he was awarded an M.Litt. by Bristol University for his dissertation on The Staging of the Cornish Miracle Plays. He has written over forty books for schools and his many radio programmes include a series, produced for the I.B.A., on the government of Great Britain. His biographies include Rider Haggard: The Great Story-Teller and The Benn Inheritance.

Anna Higgins is a graduate in American Literature of the University of East Anglia. She is a photographer and writer of many children's books, which have been translated into several European languages.

Both have travelled extensively in Europe, Africa and North America. They have three sons and live in Suffolk.

To
CESAR RAMOS HERNANDEZ -
who could not make this trip

Acknowledgements

We are grateful for the help we received from the French Government Tourist Office in London, Relais & Châteaux, Châteaux et Demeures de Tradition, Château Accueil, La Castellerie, Châteaux Hôtels Indépendants, Les Etapes Francois Coeur, Relais du Silence, International Leading Association, Gîtes de France and Minotels France Accueil. Like anyone writing about châteaux, we also acknowledge our debt to the pioneer in the field, Philippe Couderac, author of La Vie de Châteaux.

Wishing to be both consistent and totally independent, we neither asked for nor accepted free accommodation at any of the châteaux in this guide-book. With only two exceptions, we were well received by the proprietors or managers of all the châteaux we visited. We were most impressed by the kindness and consideration of the people we met, including those who spoke no English. We give them all our thanks.

Front Cover: Château d'Esclimont (55 in this guide).

Staying in the

Châteaux Hotels of Western France

Syd and Anna Higgins

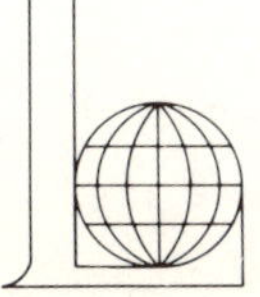

Roger Lascelles, **Cartographic and Travel Publisher**
47 York Road, Brentford, Middlesex TW8 0QP Telephone: 01-847 0935

Publication Data

Title	Staying in the Châteaux Hotels of Western France
Typeface	Phototypeset in Compugraphic Palacio
Photographs	Syd & Anna Higgins; the proprietors of châteaux.
Printing	Kelso Graphics, Kelso, Scotland
ISBN	0 903909 81 2
Edition	First Jan 1989, Second Jan 1990
Publisher	Roger Lascelles 47 York Road, Brentford, Middlesex, TW8 OQP.
Copyright	Syd & Anna Higgins

Distribution

Africa:	South Africa —	Faradawn, Box 17161, Hillbrow 2038
Americas:	Canada —	International Travel Maps & Books, P.O. Box 2290, Vancouver BC V6B 3W5.
	U.S.A. —	Boerum Hill Books, P.O. Box 286, Times Plaza Station, Brooklyn, NY 11217, (718-624-4000)
Asia:	Hong Kong —	The Book Society, G.P.O. Box 7804, Hong Kong 5-241901
	India —	English Book Store, 17-L Connaught Circus/P.O. Box 328, New Delhi 110 001
	Singapore —	Graham Brash Pte Ltd., 36-C Prinsep St.
Australasia	Australia —	Rex Publications, 413 Pacific Highway, Artarmon NSW 2064. 428 3566
Europe:	Belgium —	Brussels - Peuples et Continents
	Germany —	Available through major booksellers with good foreign travel sections
	GB/Ireland —	Available through all booksellers with good foreign travel sections.
	Italy —	Libreria dell'Automobile, Milano
	Netherlands —	Nilsson & Lamm BV, Weesp
	Denmark —	Copenhagen - Arnold Busck, G.E.C. Gad, Boghallen, G.E.C. Gad
	Finland —	Helsinki — Akateeminen Kirjakauppa
	Norway —	Oslo - Arne Gimnes/J.G. Tanum
	Sweden —	Stockholm/Esselte, Akademi Bokhandel, Fritzes, Hedengrens. Gothenburg/Gumperts, Esselte Lund/Gleerupska
	Switzerland —	Basel/Bider; Berne/Atlas; Geneve/Artou; Lausanne/Artou: Zurich/Travel Bookshop

Contents

Page
Introduction 6
Using the Guide 8
Map of the Châteaux 12
List of Châteaux 13

NORMANDY 18
BRITTANY 45
PAYS DE LA LOIRE 65
CENTRE 78
POITOU-CHARENTES 138
LIMOUSIN 151
AQUITAINE 153
MIDI-PYRENEES 178

Indexes
1. Index of Châteaux 199
2. Index of Places 203
3. Index of Châteaux with particular facilities........ 207

Introduction

What is a château? Is it a castle, a palace, a mansion, a stately home, a large country house, or a vineyard estate?

'Château' is a word used in France to describe all of these, as well as other less impressive buildings. A quick flick through this book will show the apparent infinite variety of places that are called châteaux. Of those that now exist, several were built in the eleventh century, while a couple are less than twenty years old. Some contain dozens of rooms, others only a few. There are châteaux in estates of several hundred acres; there are one or two that have only a small garden. The only generalisation that can be made about them all is that they have a stone or brick facade and almost always some form of fortification, even if it is purely decorative. Almost all are in the countryside and occupy sites that for centuries belonged to one or other of the French aristocratic families. Many châteaux either changed hands or were badly damaged during the French Revolution. With the Restoration, a large number of châteaux were either rebuilt or radically reconstructed.

So how did we make our selection? Our intention was that this guide-book should be as comprehensive as possible. We spent many months tracking down every place we could find that offered accommodation and was either called a château or looked like a château. Having completed our preliminary research, we discovered that there were over three hundred châteaux in France accepting paying guests. To cover them adequately, we decided to write two guide-books - one dealing with the châteaux in the western part of France and the other with those in the east. We then set off on several exciting tours of France, visiting, staying at and eating in an enormous variety of châteaux. The accommodation that is offered varies considerably in quality, quantity and price. Many of the places are family homes that accept a few paying guests for bed-and-breakfast. In these, the bedrooms may have changed little in the last hundred years - the furnishings are often precious antiques, the floors are highly polished oak boards, and the plumbing may well be archaic. There are also family-run châteaux that are, in everything but name, medium-sized hotels but, because officially they only accept paying guests and offer table d'hôte, they are considered to be private homes and thus avoid government regulations, inspection and price-controls. Other châteaux have been expensively converted into luxury hotels. Some of these successfully maintain the spirit and atmosphere of the ancient building, while others are as bland and anonymous as any other international hotel.

Inevitably, we have failed to discover every chateau, but of those we did encounter the only ones we have omitted from our guide are a couple of brand-new hotels which, without any justification, have been given the name 'château'. The rest are all included - the good, the average, the poor and the awful. Subject to the law of libel, we describe everywhere as we found it. Of course our view is subjective - what we hate, others may love. Of course we have prejudices - we dislike, for example, plastic flowers, cheap reproduction furniture masquerading as genuine antiques, and all carpets, wallpaper and fabrics with a swirling pattern in garish colours.

Times are changing in rural France. Every month sees châteaux being opened to paying guests for the first time. In some cases it's because the owners are finding it difficult to maintain the old family home; in others a derelict house has been purchased and restored to make it into a hotel. Every year, some château-hôtels change hands; every year a few châteaux close for good. We shall endeavour to keep up-to-date with these changes, but for subsequent editions of this guide-book to be as accurate and useful as possible we need your help. Please send us your views and comments on any châteaux you visit, whether ones already in the guide or others that you feel ought to be included.

The Second Edition

This fully revised second edition includes half a dozen new entries which replace those of châteaux that have closed since the original guide was compiled. In addition, there are rewritten entries for several other châteaux that in the last year have changed hands and been completely renovated. Many smaller changes have also been recorded — additional rooms, a different chef or the opening of a new swimming pool.

Astonishingly, there have been very few increases in the prices of accommodation — partly as a result of the French government's decision to reduce the level of VAT levied on guests staying in all but the luxury hotels. Of course, this change does not affect private châteaux accepting paying-guests.

Using this Guide

The guide-book is divided into regions, where the châteaux are listed according to their department. All the regions in the west of France are covered, and arranged in order from north to south. At the end of the book there are several indexes, including alphabetical lists of the location and name of each château. There are other indexes of châteaux that have special facilities (such as swimming-pools) or are close to one of the autoroutes. A map giving the location of each château follows this introduction.

The heading

Many châteaux are in villages too small to have been allocated a postal number (or zip-code). When this is the case, the heading gives the location of the château in capitals, with the place used as the postal address in small type:

e.g. AUDRIEU - Tilly-sur-Seulles

The heading also gives the region in capitals and the district in small type:

e.g. NORMANDY - Calvados

The château

The name of the château is preceded by its reference number and followed by an identification of the type of accommodation offered:

e.g 1 CHATEAU D'AUDRIEU H

The accommodation is graded:

H = Hotel (subject to French Government regulations)

PG = private home accepting Paying Guests

Our rating of the château

Two types of symbols are used:

⛉ showing the degree of authenticity and sense of
⛉⛉ château life
⛉⛉⛉

★ showing the degree of modern comforts and the range
★★ of facilities
★★★

In addition, we have identified the following châteaux as having a special quality or excellence:

- 27 Château du Quengo 🛡🛡🛡
- 38 Château des Briottieres 🛡🛡🛡 ★
- 42 Château du Plessis 🛡🛡 ★★
- 55 Château d'Esclimont 🛡🛡🛡 ★★★
- 68 Château des Réux 🛡🛡🛡 ★★
- 105 Château de Régagnac 🛡🛡🛡 ★
- 126 Château du Crozillat 🛡🛡🛡 ★★
- 131 Château de la Treyne 🛡🛡🛡 ★★

Like the complete collection, the châteaux in our list of the current top-eight are very varied. A couple are among the most expensive, while Quengo is one of the cheapest châteaux; Crozillat has only five guest-rooms, while Esclimont has fifty-four. Each, however, has extraordinary charm and appeal.

When open

It is not unusual for French hotels, especially those run by a well-known chef, to close for one day every week, except perhaps in high season. Many châteaux are cold, draughty places in winter and so sensibly they are then closed. A few château-hôtels near Paris are not open in August.

Prices of rooms

The prices of rooms in hotels are fixed by the French Government and depend on the size, the bathroom facilities, the view and the furnishings. Proprietors accepting paying guests into their own homes can in theory charge what they like. There is no regulation on restaurant prices - and there is a tendency for them suddenly to increase during the high season. Rather than give the exact prices supplied by each of the château, we have used in the guide letters to represent 200FF (or approximately £20):

A = 1-200FF (up to £20)
B = 201-400FF (up to £40)
C = 401-600FF (up to £60)
D = 601-800FF (up to £80)
E = 801-1000FF (up to £100)
F = 1001-1220FF (up to £120) etc.

So, for example,

Total number of rooms: 28 C-F

means that the prices of the 28 rooms are between 401FF and 1200FF. Unless otherwise stated, the costs are for a double room for one night.

In many places it is possible, on payment of a small surcharge, to have an extra bed in a room for a child. In most hotels, what is called a suite is really two connected bedrooms with a common bathroom. Some of the more expensive châteaux do have suites that consist of a bedroom and a lounge. In this guide, if a châteaux is shown as having an apartment, it will be a group of rooms including a kitchenette that can usually be rented only by the week.

Breakfast is provided by all châteaux, including those without a restaurant. In a few cases - all noted in the details of the château - breakfast is included in the cost of accommodation. Elsewhere, proprietors usually assume that guests will purchase breakfast, but be warned - the cost and what is provided vary considerably. In some places, breakfast is a rip-off. It is extremely galling to be charged 50FF for a luke-warm coffee and a stale croissant. So, in all but first-class hotels, check the night before what is provided for breakfast and, if you don't think it's likely to be good value, say you don't want it. Few châteaux are very far away from a bar or a café where an excellent breakfast can be bought at a much more reasonable price.

In châteaux where there is a restaurant, it is usually possible to have demi-pension (and three or four places accept guests only on this basis). Often a minimum length of stay is demanded. The charge shown for demi-pension is per person, although it is normally available only to a couple sharing a room.

Credit cards

Although most hotels accept some credit cards, few accept them all and many are reluctant to take any. Few private homes will accept credit cards. If in doubt, check first.

Directions

We wasted many hours driving around in search of well-hidden châteaux throughout France. Even the directions given by the owners were usually inadequate. We have tried to give detailed directions for all entries in this guide, usually from the nearest large town.

Reservations

Of course, it is possible to drive up to a château and ask if a room is available. At many times in the year, you'll certainly find something, although it may cost more than you had expected to pay. But it isn't an advisable thing to do. Many châteaux are miles off the beaten track and, like hotels throughout France, most of them will not have spare rooms in July and August. If your journey is well planned, by all means write. If a room is booked sufficiently far in advance, a deposit will be required. Having written at least once to all the châteaux in this book, we have sadly to report that a small percentage of our letters did not arrive. We found that the most satisfactory way of making a reservation was by telephone. It costs very little and an answer is immediately obtained. You will be asked to give your expected time of arrival. If, for any reason, you find that you're going to be late, ring the château, otherwise you may find that your reservation has been cancelled.

It is often easier to find a hotel room than it is a table at a restaurant. Even for a place with a modest reputation, it is advisable to make a reservation. At the best restaurants, it may be necessary to book weeks in advance. But it's always worth telephoning to find out. Cancellations do occur. The most difficult time is Sunday lunch, when many French families set off for gastronomic outings to the countryside and fixed-priced tourist menus totally disappear.

Tips

In the hotels and restaurants of France, unlike most of those in the United States and some in the United Kingdom, it is usual for a 10% or 15% service charge to be added to (or included in) the cost of a meal.

We do not approve of this practice, especially as there's no guarantee that the additional charge is distributed among the staff who are actually providing the service. The argument usually presented in favour of service charges is that they prevent customers and waiters from being embarrassed by tipping. It does no such thing because, at least in first-class hotels, tips are still expected, in addition to the iniquitous catch-all service charge.

When we discussed the matter of tipping with the managers of several first-class or luxury hotels, all stated that their staff expect tips and that the minimum amounts paid by customers satisfied with the service are:

for the waiter (lunch or dinner) — 30FF, left at the table

for baggage delivered to or collected from the room — 10FF

for the rest of the staff — 50FF, on paying the final bill.

In hotels that are not classified as 'luxury', it is assumed that tips will be given only for additional or special services, which unfortunately includes, if you're lucky enough to find anyone willing to do it, the carrying of baggage to the bedroom.

However, unless you've really been impressed by the service or have money to burn, we recommend parsimony.

We also suggest that it's sensible to check all bills. On two occasions during our tour of the châteaux in this guide, we discovered that we'd been overcharged.

Driving in France

Many guide-books contain pages of advice and instruction for foreign motorists travelling in France. We'll keep ours simple.

Take your time. France is a huge and fascinating country. Enjoy it. Never overestimate the distance you can travel in a day.

Use the country roads. Even during the high season, it is possible to drive in France along almost deserted, but adequate minor roads that pass through delightful countryside. To reach many of the châteaux in this book, you have no alternative but to chose the roads less travelled by.

Fill up with petrol when you have the opportunity. Off the autoroutes, garages, like shops, are liable to close for long lunchtimes, some part of the weekend, and on public holidays.

Have a good road map open in the car. In rural areas of France it is not unusual to find stretches of road completely closed because of road-repairs, cycle-races, accidents, film-making or religious festivals. Diversion signs are not always reliable. If you're unsure of where to go, stop and refer to your map.

Let them overtake. Everybody driving in France will have come across the lunatic who seems desperate to establish contact between the bumper of his vehicle and the exhaust-pipe of yours. Periodically, and usually just before a blind-bend or when a stream of traffic is approaching, this king-of-the-road will try to overtake. The only sensible way to deal with such people is to pull over as soon as possible and let them pass.

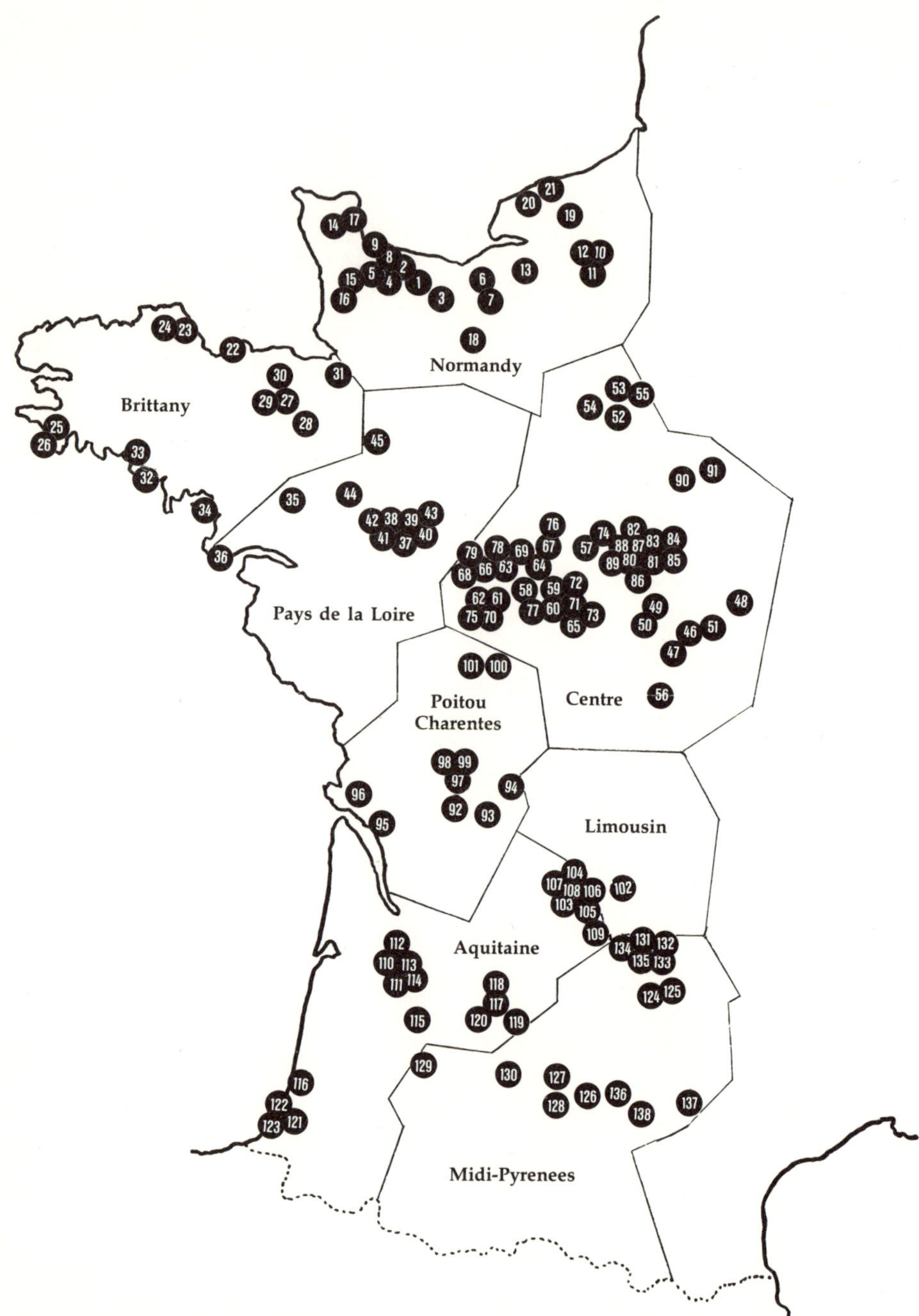

The Châteaux Hotels of Western France. The numbers on the above map refer to châteaux described in this guide.

List of Chateaux

NORMANDY

Calvados

1 Audrieu, Château d'Audrieu
2 Bayeux, Le Castel
3 Bretteville-sur-Laize, Château des Riffets
4 Le Breuil-en-Bessin, Château de Goville
5 Le Molay-Littry, Château du Molay
6 Le Pré d'Auge, Château du Pré d'Auge
7 Meulles, Hostellerie du Château de Montfort
8 Tour-en-Bessin, Château de Vaulaville
9 Vaumicel, Château de Vaumicel

Eure

10 Bazincourt-sur-Epte, Château de la Râpée
11 Douains, Château de Brécourt
12 Rosay-sur-Lieure, Le Château de Rosay
13 Tourville, Château La Ricardière

Manche

14 Bricquebec, Hôtel du Vieux Château
15 Hebecrevon, Château de la Roque
16 Montpinchon, Château de la Salle
17 Quinéville, Château de Quinéville

Orne

18 Gacé, Castel Morphée

Seine-Maritime

19 Bézancourt, Château du Landel
20 Ecrainville, Château de Diane
21 Tocqueville-en-Caux, Château de Rainfreville

BRITTANY

Côtes-du-Nord

22 Notre Dame le Guildo, Château du Val d'Arguenon
23 Pléhédel, Château Hôtel de Coatguelen
24 Pommerit-Jaudy, Château de Kermezen

Finistère

25 Plomelin, Château de Kerambleiz
26 Pont-l'Abbé, Château de Kernuz

Ille-et-Vilaine

27 Irodouer, Château du Quengo
28 Janzé, Château La Franceule
29 Landujan, Château de Léauville
30 Pleugueneuc, Château de la Motte Beaumanoir
31 Saint-Ouen-la-Rouerie, Château des Blosses

Morbihan

32 Erdeven, Château de Keraveon
33 Hennebont, Château de Locguénolé
34 Pointe de Pen-Lan, Domaine de Château de Rochevilaine

PAYS DE LA LOIRE

Loire-Atlantique

35 Châteaubriant, Hostellerie de la Ferrière
36 La Baule, Castel Marie Louise

Maine-et-Loire

37 Blaison, Château de Cheman
38 Champigne, Château des Briottières
39 Cheffes-sur-Sarthe, Château de Teildras
40 Echemiré, Château de la Grifferaie
41 Grez-Neuville, Château de la Beuvrière
42 La Jaille-Yvon, Château du Plessis
43 Montreuil-sur-Loir, Château de Montreuil

Mayenne

44 Craon, Château de Craon
45 Saint-Ouen-des-Vallons, Château de La Roche-Pichemer

CENTRE

Cher

46 Farges-Allichamps, Château de la Commanderie
47 Le Châtelet-en-Berry, Châteaux Estiveaux
48 Marseilles-les-Aubigny, Château d'Aubigny
49 Oizon, Château de la Verrerie
50 Saint-Hilaire-de-Court, Château de la Beuvrière
51 Thaumiers, Château de Thaumiers

Eure-et-Loir

52 Illiers-Combray, Château de Roussainville
53 Maillebois, Château de Maillebois
54 Nogent-le-Rotrou, Château de l'Aulnaye
55 Saint-Symphorien-le-Château, Château d'Esclimont

Indre

56 Saint-Chartier, Château de la Vallée Bleue

Indre-et-Loire

57 Amboise, Château de Pray
58 Azay-le-Rideau, Château du Gerfaut
59 Artannes-sur-Indre, Château d'Artannes
60 Artannes-sur-Indre, Château la Mothe
61 Beaumont-en-Veron, Château de Coulaine
62 Beaumont-en-Veron, Château de Danzay
63 Cinq-Mars-la-Pile, Château de Cinq-Mars
64 Joué-lès-Tours, Château de Beaulieu
65 La Celle-Guenand, Château de la Celle-Guenand
66 Langeais, Château de Chemilly
67 Larcay, Château de Larcay
68 Le Port-Boulet, Château des Réaux
69 Luynes, Domaine de Beauvois
70 Marcay, Château de Marcay
71 Montbazon, Château d'Artigny
72 Montbazon, Domaine de la Tortinière
73 Montpoupon, Château de Montpoupon
74 Nazelles, Château La Huberdière
75 Razines, Château de Milly
76 Beaumont-en-Veron, Manoir de Montour
77 Saint-Epian, Hostellerie du Château de Montgoger
78 Saint-Patrice, Hostellerie du Château de Rochecotte
79 Savigné-sur-Lathan, Château de Beaulieu

Loir-et-Cher

80 Chissay-en-Touraine, Château de Chissay
81 Couddes, Château de la Basme
82 Fréteval, Château de Rocheux
83 Huisseau-sur-Cosson, Château de Nanteuil
84 Muids-sur-Loire, Château de Colliers
85 Monthou-sur-Cher, Château du Gué-Péan
86 Montrichard, Château de la Menaudière
87 Onzain, Domaine des Hauts-de-Loire
88 Onzain, Hôtel Château des Tertres
89 Rilly-sur-Loire, Château de la Haute Borde
90 Troo, Château de la Voûte

Loiret

91 La Ferté-Saint-Aubin, Château les Muids
92 Sury-aux-Bois, Domaine de Chicamour

POITOU-CHARENTES

Charente

93 Montbron, Château Sainte-Catherine
94 Nieuil, Château de Nieuil

Charente-Maritime

95 Saint-Fort-sur-Gironde, Château des Salles

Deux-Sèvres

96 Usseau, Château d'Olbreuse

Vienne
97 Brux, Château d'Epanvilliers
98 Celle-l'Evescault, Château de la Livraie
99 Périgny, Château de Périgny
100 Sérigny, Château de Saint-Bonnet
101 Ternay, Château de Ternay

LIMOUSIN

Corrèze
102 Varetz, Château de Castel Novel

AQUITAINE

Dordogne
103 Bergerac, Château Mounet-Sully
104 Monbazillac, Château Rauly-Saulieut
105 Monterraud, Château de Régagnac
106 Montignac, Château de Puy-Robert
107 Razac-sur-l'Isle, Château de Lalande
108 Rognac, Château de Rognac
109 Veyrignac, Château de Veyrignac
Gironde
110 Barsac, Hostellerie du Château de Rolland
111 Bazas, Château d'Arbieu
112 Camiac et Saint-Denis, Château de Camiac et Saint-Denis
113 Saint-André-du-Bois, Château Malromé
114 Sauternes, Château de Commarque
Landes
115 Gabarret, Château de Buros
116 Soustons, Château Bergeron
Lot-et-Garonne
117 Monclar d'Agenais, Château Le Seiglal
118 Agen, Château Saint-Marcel
119 Saint-Nicolas de la Balerme, Château Saint-Philip
120 Tonneins, Castel Ferron
Pyrénées-Atlantiques
121 Anglet, Château de Brindos
122 Biarritz, Château du Clair de Lune
123 Bidart, Château d'Ilbarritz

MIDI-PYRENEES

Aveyron
124 Réquista, Château de Castelpers
125 Salles-Curan, Hostellerie du Levézou
Haute-Garonne
126 Caraman, Château du Crozillat
127 Larra, Château de Larra
128 Lherm, Château de Jottes
Gers
129 Cazaubon, Château Bellevue
130 Gimont-en-Gascogne, Château de Larroque

Lot

131 Lacave, Château de la Treyne
132 Loubressac, Château de Gamot
133 Rignac, Château de Roumégouse
134 Mercuès, Château de Mercuès
135 Saint-Pierre-La-Feuille, Château de Roussillon

Tarn

136 Garrevaques, Château de Garrevaques
137 Pont de l'Arn, Château de Montlédier

Tarn-et-Garonne

138 Le Pin, Château Saint-Roch

1 CHATEAU D'AUDRIEU H

🛡🛡 ★★★
Audrieu, 14250 Tilly-sur-Seulles, Calvados.
Tel: 31 80 21 52
Telex: 171 777 F
Propr: M. Gérard Livry-Level
Open: 1 Mar - 14 Dec

Twin with bath	10	C-G
Double with bath	14	C-G
Suites	4	G-H
Total rooms:	28	

No lift. 6 rooms & 2 suites on ground floor.

Restaurant: Closed Wed (lunch and dinner) and Thurs (lunch)
Chef: M. Alain Cornet
Lunch: 1230 - 1330
Dinner: 1930 - 2130
(limited service on Wed evenings for residents only)
Prix fixe: 2 menus at B
A la carte available
Demi-pension C-F

Seminars: max. 20
Groups: max. 40
Credit cards:
Eurocard
Mastercard
Visa
English spoken

Swimming pool
Tennis courts 3km
Horse riding 10km
Golf course 19km

Relais & Châteaux

13km south-east of Bayeux. From there, take the N13 towards Caen. After 10 km turn right on the D158 towards Tilly-sur-Seulles and passing through Audrieu, The château is well sign-posted and is on the left just after the village. **Airport:** *Caen-Carpiquet (8km).* **Station:** *Caen (18km)*

In some hotels the guests seem to tip-toe around and speak in hushed whispers as though they'd stumbled unexpectedly into a church - Château d'Audrieu is one such place. It is, after all, an expensive and, therefore, exclusive hotel.

Tucked away off the beaten-track, it is set in a wooded 50-acre estate. The long drive, lined with neatly-trimmed ornamental bushes, leads towards the elegant stone-built château, which has an imposing central section and two outstretched wings. However welcoming this may look, guests cannot enter the open gates leading to the vast, enclosed courtyard. A chain bars the way. The drive swings round the outer wall and along the side of the hotel where, through what might be a tradesman's entrance, guests pass into the small but elegant reception area.

The present house was completed at the beginning of the eighteenth century, but tradition has it that the first building on the site was constructed over 900 years ago by de Percy, the personal chef of William the Conqueror. He stayed in England and from him is descended the illustrious Percy family, the Dukes of Northumberland. In Normandy, the Château d'Audrieu passed through marriage to other families. At the time of the Revolution, it was owned by Camille Léonor, who fought in the army of the Prince of Condé. The Republic seized the property and sold it, but at the Restoration it was returned to Léonor. But he was the last Baron d'Audrieu. As he had no son, his property passed on his death to his daughter, Henrietta. From her, the present owners are descended.

They were fortunate to have a château to inherit. After the D-Day landings in 1944, Audrieu was for six weeks in no man's land, with British and Canadian forces on one side and a German Panza division on the other. Fortunately, the main brunt of the bombing was taken by the beech trees, some of which still carry the scars. Despite being hit by twenty-seven 105 mm shells and numerous anti-tank shells, the building survived the onslaught intact. So did the antique furniture, although when Gérard Livry-Level's father returned after the battle he found it being loaded on to carts by the victorious allied soldiers. He persuaded them to return it and now many of these exquisite pieces decorate the hotel's rooms.

The rest of the furnishings are comfortable, if not always to our taste. In many of the bedrooms there are heavily-patterned fabrics on bedspreads and canopies, though the more recently decorated rooms are simpler. The dining room is stylish, though dominated by its gold and green carpet. The food is excellent. The chef, Alain Cornet, deserves his Michelin rosette. Using home-grown vegetables and herbs, he successfully combines innovation and traditional recipes to produce memorable meals, if not overgenerous portions.

2 LE CASTEL PG

♥♥★
7 rue de la Cambette,
14400 Bayeux, Calvados.
Tel: 31 92 05 86
Propr: Baron & Baronne A. de Ville d'Avray
Open: 1 Apr - 31 Oct

Twin with bath 2 B
Double with bath 1 B
(inc. breakfast)
Total rooms: 3
Apartment: 1 (max. 5)

No lift. All bedrooms are up two flights of stairs.

No restaurant
Groups: max. 10
No credit cards
English spoken
Tennis courts 1km
Golf course 6km
Les Etapes Francois Coeur
Château Accueil

Rue de la Cambette is very narrow and easy to miss. It leads from the ring-road (directly opposite the D572 to Vers and Saint-Lô) to Rue Saint-Loup (which also joins the ring-road). At both ends of the street are signs which appear to prohibit entry. In fact they show that the road is for access only. When arriving at Bayeux by the RN13 from Paris, turn left at the end of the dual carriageway into Boulevard Montgomery. Follow the ring road past the station and over the river l'Aure. Rue de la Cambette is the second turn on the right after the river. If you miss it, take the right turn immediately afterwards - this is Rue Saint-Loup. Rue de Cambette is then the first turn on the right. Enter Le Castel through a large gateway into the courtyard, where cars can be parked. **Airport:** *Caen-Carpiquet (18km)* **Station:** *Bayeux.*

Just a stone's throw away from Bayeux cathedral and the bustle of a major tourist town, Le Castel has a beautiful and tranquil walled-garden of almost three acres, filled with carefully maintained flower-beds and overhanging trees. The three-storeyed house is finely proportioned. It was built in the middle of the eighteenth century for the knight, Fréard du Castel.

From the road, neither the house nor the garden can be seen. The only way in is through an arched gateway that leads into a small cobbled courtyard which was originally at the back of the house. From here, guests pass through a heavy wooden door into the stone-floored entrance hall that is elegantly decorated with gilt mirrors, old paintings and fresh-flowers. To the left is the impressive stone staircase and ahead, through the glass double-doors, is the garden.

More noticeable than all this, however, is the warmth of the welcome. When we arrived, Baron and Baronne de Ville d'Avray had been called away on family business, but Geoffrey, their son, entertained us royally. In moments we were sitting on the carefully raked forecourt, sipping iced drinks and chatting happily as though we'd just dropped in on close friends. Our bedroom was delightful. At a corner of the house, it had windows on two sides overlooking the garden. There were oriental rugs on the royal blue, fitted carpet. By the windows was an elegant, antique writing-desk. On the walls was a pretty blue wallpaper. The curtains and bedspread were a matching, deeper blue. The bed was comfortable and everywhere was immaculate.

The other bedrooms and the apartment are well-furnished. Off the stairs on the middle floor is an impressive sitting-room where the Baron and Baronne sometimes entertain their guests. Breakfast can be taken in the bedroom, in the garden, or in the guests' dining room on the ground-floor. If guests require it, advice will be given on where to dine and what sights to see in the area. Even though the house is filled with precious family antiques, children are genuinely welcomed. With such a large, walled garden, it's a place where children of all ages can play in perfect safety.

The proprietors state, 'Ce château n'est pas un hôtel mais une demeure recevant des hôtes payants.' It would be more accurate to say, 'This is not a hotel but a magnificent home where paying guests are received as though they were friends.'

BRETTEVILLE-SUR-LAIZE NORMANDY - Calvados

3 CHATEAU DES RIFFETS PG

★
14680 Bretteville-sur-Laize, Calvados.
Tel: 31 23 53 21, 31 95 62 14
Propr: M. Alain Cantel
Open: All year
Double with shower 2 B
Double with bath 3 B
(inc. breakfast)
Suite 1 C
Total rooms: 6

Table d'hôte (res. only) A
Chef: M. Alain Cantel
Dinner 1900 - 2100
Demi-pension B
Specialities: Normandy dishes - *tarte à la rhubarbe, gratins de poires.*

No lift.

Groups: max. 12
Seminars: max. 20
No credit cards
English & German spoken

Yoga courses (in English with vegetarian food)
Tennis courts 500m
Swimming pool 15km
Sea 25km

Gîtes de France

19km south of Caen. From there, take the N158. After 15km, at the village of La Jalousie, turn right on to the D23. At the entry to Bretteville, turn right on to the D2335. The access road to the château is almost immediately on the left. (On the left, a little further along the D23, at the junction with the D183, are the ruins of a much older château. If you see it, you've gone too far!) **Airport:** *Caen-Carpiquet (22km)* **Station:** *Caen (19km)*

Bretteville-sur-Laize is on a tributary of the River Orne at the edge of the Cinglais Forest. The countryside around is pretty and off the normal tourist beat.

Château des Riffets stands on a wooded hill overlooking the village. Rebuilt after the Second World War, it was purchased in 1983 by Alain Cantel and his wife. Since then they have spent the winter months renovating the house and outbuildings. The work is nearly complete and has been a great success. The spacious entrance hall is tiled in black and white marble. A wide staircase leads to the tastefully decorated bedrooms, which have fabric-covered walls and delightful views. There is an easy-going, welcoming atmosphere in the château. The proprietors speak excellent English and are entertaining hosts. Breakfast is taken at a long refectory table in the dining room, where there are also comfortable chairs in which guests can relax. In the extensive grounds, there are some swings for children, and growing in the uncut grass are many wild flowers, including orchids, scabious and ox-eye daisies. A pleasant country retreat.

LE BREUIL-EN-BESSIN - Le Molay-Littry NORMANDY - Calvados

4 CHATEAU DE GOVILLE H

⛉ ★★
Le Breuil-en-Bessin, 14330 Le Molay-Littry, Calvados.
Tel: 31 22 19 28, 31 22 90 80
Propr: M. Jean-Jacques Vallée
Open: 1 Feb - 5 Jan

Twin with shower	1 B
Twin with bath	12 B
Double with bath	2 B
Suite (max. 3)	1 C
Total rooms:	16

No lift

Restaurant: Open daily
Chef: M. David Sens
Lunch: 1200 - 1430
Dinner: 1900 - 2200
Prix fixe 1 menu at A
A la carte available
Demi-pension (4 days+) B
Specialities: *Terrine de truite, tourte Normande, Poulet a la mode de Bayeux.*

Groups: max. 25
Credit cards: Visa
English & Italian spoken

Antique showroom
Squash court
Exercise room
Tennis courts 1.5km
Golf course 16km
Horse riding 8km

Les Etapes Francois Coeur
La Castallerie

11km west of Bayeux. From there, take the D5. The château is on the left. The entrance is easy to miss. Watch out for the 'Antique' signs. **Airport:** *Caen-Carpiquet (29km)* **Station:** *Bayeux (11km)*

From the outside, the château has the air of a comfortable, slightly dilapidated English country house. The gardens are informal and somewhat overgrown. Friendly dogs wander along the gravel paths. Yet the interior belies this first impression. The attractive entrance hall leads to a powder-blue and pink dining room, a peach sitting-room, and a bottle-green salon with burning log-fire and baby grand piano. Each of the rooms has its own atmosphere with furnishings, curtains and carpets carefully selected and exquisitely arranged. On every flat surface there are collections of fascinating bric-à-brac. On the walls are many paintings and ornamental plaques. There are beautiful fresh flowers everywhere. Each of the bedrooms is differently decorated, but all are furnished with choice antiques and appropriate objets d'art.

The proprietor, M. Jean-Jacques Vallée, and his aide, M. Michot, are antique dealers and have a showroom in the outbuildings. Over the last few years they have renovated and totally redecorated the château. They cannot be faulted on their attention to detail, although, for some tastes, the variety of colour schemes may be a little over the top. Both men are charming and helpful hosts. Even tea is served with style - silver tray, dainty old china and delicious home-made cakes. Dinner is an occasion and the food tastes as good as it looks.

M. Vallée is rightly proud of his château. It has been in his family for generations. In 1813, Auguste Carité and his wife, Angélique, inherited the estate. Twelve years later they began building the present château, creating around it a park in the English style. It was one of their grand-daughters, Thérèse, who was given Château de Goville on 15 May 1920 as a dowry when she married Léo Vallée. After her husband's death, she retired to Goville. During the Second World War, the building survived the bombardment, but was much damaged during the occupation. Thérèse lived to be a hundred, dying in 1978. It was then that Jean-Jacques Vallée took over the estate, becoming only the fourth owner in the hundred and sixty-three years since the château was built.

5 CHATEAU DU MOLAY H

★★★
Route d'Isigny, 14330 Le Molay-Littry, Calvados.
Tel: 31 22 90 82
Direc: M. Jean Pierre Jouve
Open: 1 Mar - 30 Nov

Twin with bath	18 C
Double with bath	20 C
Total rooms:	38

Lift

Restaurant: Open daily Chef: M. Dominique Bregeault
Lunch: 1200 - 1400
Dinner: 1900 - 2200
Prix fixe: 2 menus at A
A la carte available
Demi-pension (3 days+) B-C
Specialities: lobster & langoustine, Normandy dishes.

Facilities for seminars
Groups: max. 65

Credit cards:
Am Ex, Diners Club
Eurocard, Visa
English & German spoken
Swimming pool
Tennis courts
Beauty centre & sauna
Golf course 15km
Châteaux Hôtels Indép.

16km west of Bayeux. From there, take the D5. After 14km, at the village of le Molay-Littry, turn right, (still on the D5). The château is 2km further on the left. **Airport:** *Caen-Carpiquet (30km)* **Station:** *Bayeux (16km)*

In 1758, Jacques Le Couteulx, the riding-master of Louis XV, built the first château at Molay. Seventy-five years later, the building was transformed and extended by Edouard, Comte de Chabrol-Crousol, an avid book-collector and Counsellor of State during the reign of Napolean III. For over a century, the château continued to be a family residence, but in 1940 it was requisitioned by the Germans and the sixty-acre estate was turned into a launching site for the V2 rockets aimed at Great Britain. After the war, the château became first a girls' boarding-school and then a holiday-home for Citroen employees. It became an hotel in 1978.

It is very popular and appears in many holiday brochures. Despite the trappings of a modern hotel, including the dark, wooden-panelled American Bar, we found the atmosphere redolent of an expensive boarding school. Members of staff were correct and polite, but rather formal. The bedrooms in the three-story hotel are spacious and colourful. The pleasant restaurant, 'Les Comtes de Normandie', is in a renovated wing of the house. The chef, Dominique Bregeault, presents modern versions of traditional Normandy cusine. The vast, wooded grounds are impressive, with a stream and small deer park.

LE PRE D'AUGE - Cambremer NORMANDY - Calvados

6 LE CHATEAU DE PRE D'AUGE PG

♕♕	Double (shared bath) 3 A	English spoken
Le Pré d'Auge, 14340	(inc. breakfast)	Tennis courts 4km
Cambremer, Calvados.	No lift	Riding 15km
Tel: 31 32 21 12		Sea 28km
Propr: Mme de Russe	No restaurant	
Open: Jul and Aug	No credit cards	Gîtes de France

Le Pré d'Auge is a small village, 6.5km west of Lisieux. It can be reached only by narrow roads that wind through the undulating and very beautiful countryside. The easiest way is to take the N13 from Lisieux towards Caen. After 7km, just after entering La Bosière, turn right to Le Pré d'Auge. The château is next to the church. **Airport:** *Caen-Carpiquet (54km)* **Station:** *Lisieux (7km)*

At first sight, this red-brick and white stone château seems strangely modern. This is because it has been recently reroofed with new red tiles. Yet the real age of the building can easily be seen. Part of it dates from the end of the sixteenth century. Considerable additions were made a hundred years later, giving the château a central section and two matching wings.

On a wall of the north wing is an elaborate, ancient stone sundial. The opposite wing is the oldest part of the house. In this, leading to the guests' bedrooms, is a most attractive wide staircase with wooden treads inlaid with beautiful Pré d'Auge pottery tiles for which the village was once famous. The de Russe family boasts an impressive collection of these tiles, a few dating from as early as the thirteenth century. Some have been acquired from as far afield as London auction rooms.

At the top of the staircase is a long corridor, off which are the bedrooms, the bathroom and the shared w.c. Two rooms have old-fashioned double-beds and the third has twin beds. The three bedrooms are rather small.

Breakfast is served either outside or with the family in the dining room. To reach this, guests have to walk round the outside of the house from the old wing to the front door. Mme de Russe and her son speak excellent English and are most helpful, being well informed about the history and amenities of the area.

Pottery is no longer made in the village. Indeed, apart from the château, there is little else there other than another large house and the churchyard, in which is the war-grave of a solitary Canadian, who was shot down while flying with the Royal Air Force. But the château is set among trees on a hill overlooking a beautiful, fertile valley. It is a quiet, idyllic spot, yet only a short winding road away from Lisieux and the busy N13.

MEULLES - Orbec NORMANDY - Calvados

7 HOSTELLERIE DU CHATEAU DE MONTFORT H

♁ ★ ★
Meulles, 14290 Orbec, Calvados.
Tel: 31 32 91 66
Propr: Mme Delen
Direc: M. Renault
Open: 1 Mar - 31 Dec

Twin with shower	2	B
Twin with bath	11	B
Double with bath	3	B
Twin rooms (for 4)	2	B-C
Total rooms:	18	

Lift

Restaurant: Open daily
Chef: M. Renault
Lunch: 1200 - 1430
Dinner: 1900 - 2130
Prix fixe: 3 menus at A
A la carte available
Specialities: *Viennoisé de saumon et turbot à la fondue de légumes; Oeufs de poule brouillés au petit Cormeillais; Terrine de caneton maison à la gelée de Calvados.*
Demi-pension (3 days+) B

Seminars: max. 30
Banquets: max. 80
Credit cards:
American Express
Diners Club
Eurocard
Visa
English & German spoken
Swimming pool
Tennis court
Horse riding 1km

19km south of Lisieux. From there, take the D519 to Orbec, where turn right on to the D46. Meulles is a further 8km. **Airport:** *Caen-Carpiquet (67km)* **Station:** *Lisieux (24km)*

The château was built on an ancient Roman site by the Bordeaux family. It was finished in 1880 and the first occupants were the soldiers of the invading Prussian army. A later owner was Prince Montacheff, who had been deprived of his oil-wells - if not of his entire fortune - by the Russian Revolution. During the Second World War, the German Army occupied the château. While Marshal Rommel was staying there, he was wounded.

After the war, the château was converted into a hotel. It is not an elegant building, being a jumble of red-brick and white-stone cladding. The grey slate roof is pockmarked with many windows and the steep turrets seem cut-off like broken pencils. The rooms are spacious and comfortably, if modestly, furnished. The grounds of over 12 acres are most pleasant. The surrounding countryside is delightful. On either side of the château are stud farms - one is for breeding stallions, the other for training trotting-horses.

It is the restaurant that is the château's high-point. M. Renault successfully combines the best of the old with the new, at bargain prices.

TOUR-EN-BESSIN - Bayeux NORMANDY - Calvados

8 CHATEAU DE VAULAVILLE PG

♥♥	Doubles 3 B	No credit cards
Tour-en-Bessin, 14400 Bayeux, Calvados.	Suite 1 C (inc. breakfast)	English spoken
Tel: 31 92 52 62	No en suite bathrooms	Golf course 5km
Propr: Mme Corblet de Fallerans	No lift.	Tennis courts 7km
		Sea 7km
Open: 1 Mar - 30 Oct	Table d'hôte (res. only) A	Les Etapes Francois Coeur

7.5km west of Bayeux. From there, take the N13 towards Carentan. Just after entering Tour-en-Bessin, turn right along the D100, heading towards Port-en-Bessin. The château is on the left, approached along a tree-lined drive. (It is slightly confusing that 100 m further along the N13 from the D100 turn-off there is another château very similar in appearance to Vaulaville. If you see it, you've missed the right turn!) **Airport:** *Caen-Carpiquet (25km)* **Station:** *Bayeux (7.5km)*

Built in 1720, this is a beautiful château, with a 'lived in' feel about it. A marbled entrance hall leads into an enormous sitting-room. Through the double windows that open on to a small balcony there is an idyllic rural view over a river and meadows. Breakfast is taken in this delightful room which, like the rest of the château, is furnished with delicate antiques. From the hall, a winding staircase leads to the medium-sized bedrooms which have polished wooden floors and beautiful Turkey rugs. There are wash-basins and bidets in each room. Bathrooms and toilets are shared.

Mme Corblet de Fallerans is energetic, expressive and friendly. She has many tales to tell about the German occupation during the Second World War, when at one time three hundred German soldiers were billeted in the château.

Apart from the area close to the château, the enormous grounds have been allowed to run wild and the long grass is full of wild flowers. It is an utterly peaceful spot.

9 CHATEAU DE VAUMICEL PG

Vaumicel, Vierville-sur-Mer, 14710 Trévières, Calvados.	Twin rooms with bath	1 A	No credit cards
Tel: 31 22 40 06	Double with shower	3 A	Horse-riding
Propr: Mme F. de Bellaigue	Total rooms:	4	Tennis courts 2km
	No lift		Sea 2km
Open: 1 Mar - 31 Oct	No restaurant		Gîtes de France

23km north-west of Bayeaux. From there, take the D6 to Port-en-Bessin, where turn left on to the D514, which runs westwards parallel to the coast. In the centre of Vierville-sur-Mer (just before the right turn to Omaha Beach) turn left into a narrow road, signposted to Vaumicel. The château is down the first road on the right. Look out for signs to 'Club Hippique'. **Airport:** *Caen-Carpiquet (37km)* **Station:** *Bayeux (19km)*

Without the usual tree-lined drive, this sixteenth century château looms up suddenly as you round a bend in the narrow road. At first it seems a forbidding place. Three round pointed towers flank its grey-stone, ivy-clad walls and dark grey slate covers the roof. Yet inside is pleasantly inviting - in a homely, no-nonsense way. There are flagstone floors, plain furniture, an enormous family kitchen and very friendly dogs.

Based at the château's extensive stables is Club Hippique du Vaumicel, which organises a wide range of equestrian activities and events for children and adults. There are twenty ponies, thirty horses and four carriages. These can be hired by the hour or by the day. Pony treks are arranged through the rolling countryside and along the nearby sandy beaches.

In a beautiful setting and close to the sea, Château de Vaumicel is an ideal place for an active, no-frills holiday.

BAZINCOURT-SUR-EPTE NORMANDY - Eure

10 CHATEAU DE LA RAPEE H

🛡 ★★
27140 Bazincourt-sur-Epte, Eure.
Tel: 32 55 11 61
Proprietors: M. & Mme Bergeron
Open: 1 Mar - 31 Dec
(Closed last fortnight in Aug & every Wed)
Twin with shower 4 B
Twin with bath 6 B
Total rooms: 10
Apartment: 1 (max. 4) C
No lift

Restaurant: Closed all day Wed and Tue evenings from 1 Oct to Easter.
Prix fixe: 2 menus at B
A la carte available
Demi-pension (3 days+) B
Specialities: *Tarte soufflée au Livarot; Galantine de truite, saumonée et langoustine; Anguille* (river eel) *en matelotte au cidre brut; Douillon normand* (apples in pastry).

Seminars: max. 30
Receptions: max. 100
Credit cards: Am Ex, Diners Club Eurocard, Visa
English & German spoken
Flying club 6km
Tennis courts 6km
Golf 6km
Horse riding 6km

La Castellerie
Châteaux Hôtels Indép.

5km north of Gisors. From there, take the D915 towards Gournay-en-Bray. Immediately after passing the sign for Bazincourt, turn left off the main road towards the centre of the village where, at a T-junction, turn right on to the D14. Shortly afterwards turn left. A narrow road leads to the château, which is less than a kilometre away on the left. **Airport:** *RoissyParis (72km)* **Station:** *Gisors (5km)*

The architectural style of this château is said to be 'Anglo-Norman Baroque'. It is easy to see why it didn't prove to be popular. Built in 1825, the three-storeyed building is a hotch-potch of red brick, red tiles and ornamental wood and stone.

In 1973, the Bergerons converted the property into a family-run hotel and have tried hard to make the unpromising building comfortable. All the rooms - including the bedrooms and the sun-lounge - are vast; there is much wooden panelling on the walls. To this has been added heavy antique furniture and dark brocades.

The helpful proprietors are enthusiastic and knowledgeable about Norman customs and history. This is reflected, not only in their choice of decor, but in the above average cuisine. Most of the dishes are made from regional recipes.

With a forest on one side and meadows on the other, the flower-filled grounds are delightful. It is a peaceful and secluded place to stay.

DOUAINS - Pacy-sur-Eure NORMANDY - Eure

11 CHATEAU DE BRECOURT H

🛡🛡 ★★★
Douains, 27120 Pacy-sur-Eure, Eure.
Tel: 32 52 40 50, 32 52 41 39
Telex: 172250
Propr: M. Philippe Savry
Direc: M. & Mme Charpentier
Open: All year

Single with bath	3 B
Twin with bath	6 B-D
Double with bath	12 B-D
Suites (max 4)	4 D-E
Total rooms:	25

Restaurant: Open daily
Chef: M. Rethore
Lunch: 1230 - 1330
Dinner: 1930 - 2130
Prix fixe: Menus at A & B
A la carte available
Specialities: *Jambon de canard; Salade tiède de langoustine; Escalope de turbotin; Ris de veau poêles.*

No lift.

Seminars: max. 50
Groups: max. 50
Credit cards:
Access, American Express
Diners Club, Visa
English & German spoken

Tennis courts
Indoor swimming pool
Golf course 20km

Relais et Châteaux

70km north-west of Paris. From there, take the A13 autoroute. Exit at Vernon and take the D181 south towards Pacy-sur-Eure. After 1km turn left on the D75 towards Douains. The château is 1km on the right. **Airport:** *Orly-Paris (70km)* **Station:** *Vernon (7km)*

This is an elegant château, set in 55 acres of wooded parkland that is swathed with broad walkways. Started in the seventeenth century, the building was considerably extended during the eighteenth century in the classical style typical of Louis XIII. Built of white stone and ornamented with red brick, it has a four-storeyed main section and two long symmetrical wings which step down from three storeys (including a covered walkway) to two. The fourth side of the square is walled to form a formal garden and courtyard.

Badly damaged by bombing during the Second World War, the château was meticulously restored and opened as a hotel in 1981.

The bedrooms (each with its own bathroom) are comfortable. With its large stone fireplace, its beamed ceiling, terracotta walls and subdued lighting, the dining room is a fine setting for the excellent meals produced by the chef, M. Rethore. On Friday evenings his Menu Grand Siècle is served. The eight fascinating courses are all based on the recipes of master-chefs from the eighteenth century, including Marin's *Fricandeau de Veau à la Bourgeoise.* Highly recommended!

12 LE CHATEAU DE ROSAY H

♛♛♛ ★★
27790 Rosay-sur-Lieure, Eure.
Tel: 32 49 66 51
Propr: M. Norbert Castellane
Open: 1 Apr - 1 Jan

Twin with bath	16	B
Double with bath	8	B
Suites (max. 4)	4	C
Total rooms:	28	

No restaurant
(Restaurants in the area)

Seminars: max. 50
Groups: max. 50
Receptions: max. 600

No credit cards

No lift.

English & German spoken

Fishing
Tennis courts 4km
Horse-riding 4km
Swimming pool 15km
Golf course 25km

Châteaux Hôtels Indép.
Châteaux Accueil

31km south-east of Rouen. From there, take the N14 towards Grainville. After 24km, and immediately after crossing the River Andelle, turn left on to the D321 towards Lyons-la-Forêt. Rosay-sur-Lieure is a further 7km. The drive to the château is on the left, just after passing through Rosay-sur-Lieure. **Airport:** *Boos/Rouen (30km)* **Station:** *Rouen (32km)*

In the middle of the beautiful Forest of Lyons, this large, imposing château was built at the beginning of the seventeenth century. Set in a well-kept garden, it has a long central section (built in 1611) and two small symmetrical wings that were added eight years later. With a grey-slate roof and a facade of white roughcast and decorative red brick, it is typical of the style of Louis XIII.

During the French Revolution, the resident châtelain of Rosay was left unharmed by the mob. Even more surprisingly, a unique decree of the Convention gave him the right to continue hunting so that the peasants and foresters of the area could be protected from wolves. After many years of neglect, the château and grounds were purchased in 1969 by the Castellane family. After careful restoration, the château is once again an important social and cultural centre. Used by local people for wedding receptions and cocktail parties, it is also a place where concerts and plays are presented during the summer.

The public rooms have been meticulously decorated and the painted ceilings restored; the wooden floors are highly polished; the furniture is carefully chosen antiques. The bedrooms are light and airy, painted in harmonising colours. It is a stylish retreat in the heart of beautiful countryside.

TOURVILLE - Pont-Audemer NORMANDY - Eure

13 CHATEAU LA RICARDIERE PG

♛♛ ★
Route de Lisieux, Tourville,
27500 Pont-Audemer, Eure.
Tel: 32 41 09 14
Propr: Mme Denise Carel
Open: All year

Twin with shower 1 B
Twin with bath 3 B
(inc. breakfast)
Total rooms: 4
(2 are in a half-timbered annexe.)

No lift. 2 ground-floor rooms.
No restaurant
Groups: max. 8
No credit cards
English spoken

3km south of Pont-Audemer (which is close to Autoroute 13). Leave the town by the D139 towards Lisieux. At the end of the built-up area, there is a sawmill on the left. 200 m after this, turn left on to a small private drive. In a broad sweep, it leads, by way of a small bridge over a river, to the château. **Airport:** *Deauville (35km)* **Station:** *Bernay or Lisieux*

The narrow drive winds over the small bridge and up a hill. Nuts cluster on the overhanging hazel trees and ahead lies a giant copper beech and La Ricardière. A pretty little château that nestles into the side of the hill, it was built in the Directoire style just after the French Revolution on the site of a medieval castle that had once protected the feudal village.

Two of the guest rooms are at the top of the house and are very spacious with sloping ceilings. The rooms are pleasant. The bathrooms are clean and functional. There are also two similar rooms available in the half-timbered garden-house. Breakfast which is served in the comfortable dining room, includes home-made jam. Although no other meals are available, there are many restaurants in the area.

This isolated house is surrounded by tranquil gardens and shaded by ancient trees. Through the meadows filled with wild flowers flows a small trout stream. It is a beautiful, peaceful place. The château, though simple, is most agreeable.

14 HOTEL DU VIEUX CHATEAU H

⛉ ★
4 cours du Château, 50260 Bricquebec, Manche.
Tel: 33 52 24 49
Propr: M. A & Mme H Hardy
Open: 16 Jan-21 Dec

Twin with shower	4 A
Twin with bath	12 A-B
Double with shower	1 A
Double with bath	9 B
Suites	4
Total rooms:	30

No lift, 2 gd.fl. rooms and ramps.

Restaurant: Open daily
Chef: M. Otus Denis
Lunch: 1200 - 1400
Dinner: 1930 - 2115
Prix fixe 4 menus at A
A la carte available
Demi-pension (3 days+) A
Specialities: *Brouillade royale* (scrambled eggs on toast with smoked salmon); *Supreme de saumon auc poireaux* (with leeks); *Sole sauce capre; Délice du château;* home-made sorbet.

Seminars: max. 60
Groups: max. 50
Receptions: max. 150
Credit cards:
Access
Eurocard
Visa
English, German & Italian spoken

Choral concerts in July
Tennis courts 500m
Sea 15km
Châteaux Hôtels Indép.

22km south of Cherbourg. From the ferry terminal, take the D3 and after 2.5km turn left on to the D900 to Bricquebec. The château is in the middle of the town. **Airport:** *MaupertusCherbourg (22km)* **Station:** *Valognes (11km)*

The hotel is one of the buildings within the bailey of a castle that was first fortified in the tenth century. The château was occupied by various aristocratic families, but in 1820, after the Revolution, it was sold to a resident of Bricquebec who, six years later, gave the keep and the clock-tower to the village which acquired the rest of the château this century.

The hotel is in the oldest surviving part of the château. Dating from the twelfth century, the building originally housed the vast 'Salle des Chevaliers', part of which is now the restaurant. Although the bedrooms above are small, they have accommodated many famous guests. Queen Victoria is said to have stayed there in 1857.

The hotel is run by an Australian couple. They and their staff are helpful and efficient. There is a wide choice of dishes on the menus and the food is good. There is a sitting room, a bar and a small garden. It is a friendly, simple and old-fashioned place with heavy furniture, wood panelling, leaded door-windows and tiled floors. Queen Victoria must have felt at home in the Hôtel du Vieux Château.

HEBECREVON NORMANDY - Manche

15 CHATEAU DE LA ROQUE H

⛉ ★★	Twin rooms w.shower 1 B	Seminars: max. 30
50180 Hebecrevon - Manche.	Twin with bath 5 B	Groups: max. 10
Tel: 33 57 33 20/62 63	Double with bath 1 B (inc. breakfast)	No credit cards
Telex: 171 338 F	Total rooms: 7	English spoken
Propr: M. Raymond & Mme Mireille Delisle	Apartments 2 F	Fishing
Open: All year	Table d'hôte available A	Tennis courts 1km
	Dinner only: 2000	Golf 6km
No lift	Demi-pension (2 days+) B	Sea 25km
1 ground-floor room		Gîtes de France

5km north-west of Saint-Lô. From there, take the D972 westwards towards Coutances. On the outskirts of Saint-Lô, turn right on to the D900 which passes through Hebecrevon. After the village, turn left on to the D77 towards Saint Giles. The château is on the right after 500 metres. **Airport:** *Caen (68km)* **Station:** *Saint-Lô (7km)*

As a past winner of the Tour de France cycle race, Raymond Delisle is a sporting hero. Now he and his petite wife run a small family hotel that provides excellent value and a most pleasant atmosphere.

The château, which the Delisles purchased in 1978, was built towards the end of the sixteenth century. It consists now of a long central section, which is linked to a small north wing by a tower containing a spiral staircase. At one time there was a matching south wing and tower. Local tradition has it that this part of the building was demolished in 1930, when the then owner was digging for a treasure that was never found. Another local story dates back to 1815, when the Prussian army used the château as their headquarters. Eugène La Couture, who was twenty years old, refused to sell some tobacco to a soldier. For this, he was tied to a tree in the avenue leading to the château and given a hundred lashes with a cane.

The bedrooms are pretty and overlook a beautiful valley. The bathrooms are impeccable. Breakfast and, if reserved, the evening meal are eaten at a huge refectory table in the dining room.

MONTPINCHON NORMANDY - Manche

16 CHATEAU DE LA SALLE H

⛉⛉ ★★
50210 Montpinchon, Manche.
Tel: 33 45 95 19
Propr: M. Michel & Mme Cécile Lemesle
Open: 21 Mar - 31 Oct

Twin with shower	1 B
Twin with bath	6 B
Double with bath	3 B-C
Total rooms:	10

No lift

Restaurant: Open daily Chef: M. Claude Espabens
Lunch: 1230 - 1400
Dinner: 1930 - 2130
Prix fixe: Menus at A & B
A la carte available
Demi-pension (2 days+) B
Specialities: *Le délice du Bois Marquis (foie gras* and sweetbread); *Le petit civet du pêcheur*

Seminars: max. 30
Groups: max. 20
Credit cards:
Am Ex, Diners Club, Visa
English & Spanish spoken

Swimming pool 10km
Golf 30km

Relais & Châteaux

The château is just off the D73 be-tween the two villages of Montpinchon and Cerisy-la-Salle, some 75km south of Cherbourg. Either from Coutances travel south on the D7 for 5km and then turn left on to the D73 for a further 13km; or from Saint-Lo- travel south-west on the D999 for 3.5km, turn right on to the D38 and then after 10.5km turn right on to the D73 for a further 5km. Although the roads are narrow and winding, directions to the château are well-signposted. **Airport:** *Granville (30km)* **Station:** *Coutances (18km)*

The earliest part of the château dates from the eleventh century. Five hundred years later, a granite extension was built on to this stone keep, which originally enclosed a deep pit, known locally as 'la prison'. This building became the north wing in the eighteenth century, with the construction of the main section, which is decorated with granite and red schist.

In 1968, the present owners began refurbishing the château, which had been in Mme Lemesle's family since the beginning of this century. From the outside, the ivy-covered granite building is impressive. Inside, although the expensive furnishings seem heavy and sombre, there is the refined, friendly atmosphere one associates with a favourite maiden aunt.

Justifiably, but remarkably for such a small and remote hotel, the restaurant has been awarded a Michelin rosette. As there are only ten bedrooms (all large and some with four-poster beds), it is no wonder that people wishing to stay at the château during the summer months are advised to book six weeks in advance.

17 CHATEAU DE QUINEVILLE H

⛉⛉ ★★
Quinéville, 50410
Montebourg, Manche.
Tel: 33 21 42 67
Propr: Mme Jocelyne Lemaire
Direc: Mme Monette Regnault
Open: 1 Apr - 31 Dec

Total rooms: 12 B
No lift

Restaurant: Open daily
Lunch: 1200 - 1400
Dinner: 1900 - 2100
Prix fixe: 3 menus at A
A la carte available
Demi-pension (2 days+) B
Specialities: *Crabe farci; Canard aux pommes; Andouillettes* (small smoked sausage made of chitterlings); *Coquelet a la Cotentine.*

Seminars: max. 30
Groups: max. 20
Credit cards: Visa
English spoken

Fishing
Tennis courts 500m
Sea at 600 metres

Golf course 1km
Utah Beach 10km

On the coast, 35km south-east of Cherbourg. From the ferry-terminus, take the N13 and at Montebourg take the D42 eastwards to Quinéville. The château is on the right, just after entering the village. **Airport:** *MaupertusCherbourg (28km)* **Station:** *Valognes (15km)*

The remains of a Roman fire-place, dating from the first century, still survive in the grounds of Quinéville. Close to what was once an important port, this ancient, heavily wooded estate has often been a battle-ground. On 1 April 1416, Henry V, King of England, seized the lands and gave them to one of his nobles, Thomas Burgh. Quinéville remained in English hands until 1450, when it was recaptured by the deposed Norman baron.

After the 1688 revolution in Britain, James II fled to France. On 28 April 1692, he transferred his headquarters to Quinéville. Twelve thousand of his Irish troops camped in the surrounding woods. On 2 June, James Stuart watched powerless as, just off-shore, his small fleet was defeated by the numerically superior British navy at the battle of La Hougue.

The present château was constructed in the early part of the eighteenth century. During the French Revolution, the buildings were attacked by local people. Their main grievance was the damage caused to their crops by the two thousand pigeons that nested in the château's dovecote - pigeons that before the Revolution they had been forbidden to kill. The dovecote was destroyed.

During the Second World War, the château was occupied by German soldiers. On 6 June, American troops landed at Utah beach, 10km away. Early in the morning, sixty American parachutists of the 101st Airborne Division landed and were killed at Quinéville. By 14 June, the Americans had fought their way to the château, but it was there that their northern advance was halted. Four American and nine German soldiers were killed at the château. Twenty-two shells landed on the lawn, thirteen in the main courtyard, seven in the kitchen-garden, and two on the main building.

The architectural style of this white-stone, oft-beleaguered château is classical, with elegant proportions and a charming atmosphere. It has retained many original features and the furnishings are carefully chosen to blend well with the surroundings. In the dining room, large black and white tiles complement the plain off-white panelled walls. High-backed chairs are grouped around a long refectory table. Chandeliers, candelabras and a large gilt-framed mirror add touches of luxury.

The sounds and scars of past battles have faded. The château, set in a twenty-five acre wood, is now a haven of peace.

18 CASTEL MORPHEE H

♛ ★
2 rue de Lisieux, 61230
Gacé, Orne.
Tel: 33 35 51 01
Propr: Mme Janine Lecanu
Open: 1 Mar - 31 Dec

No lift

Twin with beds 6 B
Double with shower 2 B
Suites (max. 4) 2 C
Total rooms: 10
(The four cheapest rooms are in the summer-house.)

No restaurant

Credit cards:
American Express
Diners Club, Visa
English, Italian & Spanish spoken
Billiard room
Tennis 1km

La Castellerie

51km south of Lisieux. From there, take the D519. After 28km, turn right on to the N138, which leads to Gacé. **Airport:** *Caen (76km)* **Station:** *L'Aigle (32km) or Argentan (27km)*

Situated in a small park containing many old trees (including a rare Ginkgo), Castel Morphée dates from the end of the nineteenth century. Faced with red brick and carved white stone, it is not as ugly as many châteaux built in that period. In fact it has a pleasing, neat symmetry. Only the ornamentation jars - it is a trifle too grand for what is really a small building.

The interior was also given touches of ostentation, especially in the billiard room which has heavy wooden panelling and a bulbous, carved fireplace. Above it hangs a huge wooden shield on which are splayed nine swords. The ceiling of the dining room and lounge are festooned with elaborate and gilded mouldings.

Too often, wallpaper has been used that has large, intrusive patterns. This even applies to bedrooms on the third floor which, being under the roof, have sloping ceilings. We found it overpowering. However, the furnishings are of very good quality and everywhere is immaculate. The wooded garden is attractive.

BEZANCOURT - Gournay-en-Bray NORMANDY - Seine-Maritime

19 CHATEAU DU LANDEL H

♡♡ ★★
Bézancourt,
76220 Gournay-en-Bray,
Seine Maritime.
Tel: 35 90 16 01
Propr: M. Pierre Cardon
Open: 15 Mar - 15 Nov

Twin with shower	2 B
Twin with bath	15 B
Total rooms:	17
No lift	

Restaurant: Closed Sun eves and every Mon
Chef: M. V. Cardon (the proprietor's son)
Lunch: 1230 - 1400
Dinner: 1930 - 2200
Prix fixe: 1 menu at A
A la carte available
Demi-pension (3 nights+) B
Specialities: *Fonds d'artichauts pochés au saumon rose; Escargots sautés aux petits lardons; Magret de canard a la gelée de groseilles.*

Seminars: max. 50
Groups: max. 30
Receptions: max. 80
Credit cards: Visa
English spoken

Tennis courts
Swimming pool 500m
Horse riding 1km
Golf course 20km

Châteaux Hôtels Indép.

42km east of Rouen. From there, take the N21 towards Gournay-en-Bray. After 36km (3km after La Feuillie), turn right on to the D62 to Bézancourt. In the centre of the village turn right on to the D401 (which soon becomes the D4), towards Lyons-la-Forêt. The château is 3km further on the left. **Airport:** *BoosRouen (40km)* **Station:** *Gournay-en-Bray (12km)*

At the edge of the Forest of Lyons, this large and impressive château stands in a park of 135 acres. Some of it is a manicured lawn, but most is woodland where many wild animals, including deer, roam freely.

Unspoiled by the odd-shaped extensions at either end, the Château du Landel has a delightful, classical simplicity. It was built in the mid eighteenth century, not as a gentleman's residence, but as a glass-factory. Since the fifth century, glass had been manufactured on the site, where all the necessary raw materials could be found. There was wood in abundance for fuel, ferns for the ash, and in the river was fine sand and water. The factory closed in 1870 and the estate became a dairy farm. In 1978, M. and Mme Cardon with their sons transformed the château into an hotel.

The decor of the house is a mixture of rustic and grand; it has much charm and appropriateness. In one beamed lounge is a large brick fireplace where a log-fire blazes on chilly days. In another room there is an elaborate, enamelled stove which has a flue decorated like a Corinthian column. One of the bedrooms is in the style of Louis XVI, with grey-painted wardrobe, bed and tables decorated with elaborate moulding. The bedrooms on the second floor, under the roof, are delightful, with splendid views across the park.

M. and Mme Cardon are most welcoming. Their son, Vres Cardon, is the skilful and hard-working chef. The food is delightful and modestly priced. The gilt folding-chairs in the dining room seem out-of-place.

Château du Landel is a comfortable, peaceful retreat in a remote and beautiful part of Normandy.

ECRAINVILLE NORMANDY - Seine-Maritime

20 CHATEAU DE DIANE PG

♛♛♛★	Twin with shower	3 C	Groups: max. 25
76110 Ecrainville par Goderville, Seine-Maritime.	Twin with bath	1 C	No credit cards
Tel: 35 42 64 79, 35 27 76 02	Double with shower	1 C	
Propr: Mme Diane Delahève	Double with bath	1 C	Tennis court 1km
Open: Fri - Mon every week and the whole of Aug.	Other rooms	14 B	Golf 10km
	Total rooms:	20	Horse riding 14km
			Sea 15km
	No restaurant		
No lift			Châteaux Hôtels Indép.

23km north-east of Le Havre. From there, take the D925 towards Goderville. 3km before the town, turn left on to the D68 towards Ecrainville. The entrance to the château is a further 1.5km on the left. **Airport:** *Le Havre (21km)* **Station:** *Breute-Beuzeville (3km)*

This is the most idiosyncratic of châteaux, now inseparably linked - and not just in name - to its owner, Mme Diane Delahève. She is a famous beautician who receives paying guests at weekends and in the summer in order to help her maintain her unusual home. An extraordinary and dynamic woman, she has written a Méditation sur les étoiles in which she expresses her belief that bathrooms everywhere are harmful to health and beauty. However, she provides them for her guests!

She has furnished each room with beautiful things from different periods and places. Her eclecticism is shown by the names she has given to the bedrooms, such as La Baie de Hong-Kong, Mme Chrysanthème, Les Oiseaux du Paradis, and L'Ange Blanc.

Although the château dates from the late nineteenth century, it was built somewhat in the style of Louis XIII so that it harmonised with the existing buildings, such as the pretty, circular dovecote, which was built in the eighteenth century and has been refurbished to make a romantic bedroom. Around the château is a park of 17 acres, half of which is an ancient woodland.

A most unusual experience.

TOCQUEVILLE-EN-CAUX - Bacque-en-Caux NORMANDY - Seine-Maritime

21 CHATEAU DE RAINFREVILLE PG

Tocqueville-en-Caux, 76730 Bacque-en-Caux, Seine-Maritime.
Tel: 35 85 36 16
Propr: Mme Micheline Declercq
Open: 1 May - 31 Sep

Double with bath 2 A (inc. breakfast)
No lift

No restaurant

No credit cards

Horses
Fishing 500m
Tennis 5km
Sea 15km

Gîtes de France

25km south-west of Dieppe, Rainfreville is a peaceful hamlet tucked well-away from the beaten track. From Dieppe, the easiest - though not the most direct route - is to take the N27 and after 13km, turn right on to the D23 to Bacqueville-en-Caux. In the small town, take a right turn on to the D149. After 7km, turn right on to the D2, which leads to Rainfreville. The château is on the left, just after the village sign. **Airport:** *Rouen (59km)* **Station:** *Dieppe (18km)*

This is a large, gloomy house. Like a deserted film set, it looks slightly eerie - as though something unexpected were about to happen. Enormous beech trees stand guard; ivy is growing up the walls; steep turrets jut out from the grey roof; and at the windows there are small confining balconies.

When we arrived, there was nobody at home, but eventually Madame Declercq arrived to let us in. She is a sprightly woman who has ten children and twenty-two grandchildren. Now she, her farmer-husband and one son live alone in the house.

Few changes have been made to the property over the years. There is a stone floor in the bathroom. The plumbing is quaintly antique. Our bath had lions' feet and was so deep that it was difficult to see over the edge. The water took an age to drain away. The shared w.c. is at the end of the long, dark, central corridor.

Breakfast is served in the dining room and guests are allowed to use the family lounge, where a log fire crackles on cold, windy evenings.

NOTRE DAME DU GUILDO - Saint-Cast BRITTANY - Côtes-du-Nord

22 CHATEAU DU VAL D'ARGUENON PG

♛♛ ★★
Notre Dame du Guildo, 22380 Saint-Cast, Côtes-du-Nord.
Tel: 96 41 07 03
Propr: M. and Mme de la Blanchardière
Open: 1 Mar - 12 Nov

No lift

Twin with shower	1	B
Twin with bath	1	B
Double with shower	1	B
Double with bath	1	B
Double (for 4)	1	C
Total rooms:	5	

No restaurant

Groups: max. 10
No credit cards
English spoken

Bordering the sea
Tennis court
Golf 5km

Les Etapes Francois Coeur

15km south-west of Dinard. From there, take the D168 to Ploubalay, where the road becomes the D786. Follow this for a further 8km. The château is off the road on the far side of the River Arguenon. **Airport:** *Dinard (13km)* **Station:** *Plancoet (10km)*

Built at the end of the sixteenth century in a delightful spot overlooking the estuary of the River Arguenon, the château was acquired some decades later by the Marquise de Moussay as a summer home. She was a Protestant and Louis XIV ordered that she should either be beheaded or recant on her knees in the Parliament Square of Rennes. Sensibly, she chose survival.

At the beginning of the eighteenth century, the house was purchased by the Morvonnais family, from whom the present proprietors are descended. It was one of their grandfathers who finally obtained the permission for Châteaubriand to be buried on the island of Grand Be at Saint Malo.

The château is still very much a private home, full of the portraits and possessions of previous generations. The agreeable bedrooms are furnished in different styles. The building itself, which consists of two stone wings at right angles, appears somewhat bleak, but in the 30-acre grounds there is a pretty circular dovecote and an old chapel, both dating from the fifteenth century.

Château du Val d'Arguenon is a pleasant place to stay for a night or two.

23 CHATEAU HOTEL DE COATGUELEN H

♔♔♔ ★★★
Pléhédel, 22290 Lanvollon, Côtes-du-Nord.
Tel: 96 22 31 24
Telex: 741 300 F
Propr: Marquis de Boisgelin
Direc: Mme N. de Morchoven
Open: 1 Apr to 4 Jan

Twin with shower	1	D
Twin with bath	5	D-E
Double with shower	1	C
Double with bath	6	D-E
Suites (max. 3)	3	F
Total rooms:	16	

No lift

Restaurant: closed Tues and Wed lunchtimes
Chef: M. Louis Le Roy (author of *La Cuisine Bretonne d'aujourd'hui* and *La Cuisine Tonique)*
Lunch: 1200 - 1400
Dinner: 1930 - 2130
Prix fixe: Menus at A & B
A la carte available
Demi-pension C-D
Specialities: *Salade de langoustines; Filet de bar* (bass) *dans sa robe de laitue; Contrefilet cuit dans sa croute de sel; Feuilleté aux poires.*

Seminars: max. 30
Groups: max. 30
Credit cards:
American Express
Diners Club
Mastercard
Visa
English spoken

Swimming pool
Tennis courts
Equestrian centre
Trout fishing
9-hole golf course
Sea 7km

Relais & Châteaux

33km north-west of Saint Brieuc. From there, take the D6 towards Paimpol. After the by-pass round Lanvollon, the road becomes the D7. The château is 5km further on the left. **Airport:** *Saint Brieuc (26km)* **Station:** *Paimpol (10km)*

This is a hotel of charm and distinction on which considerable care and expense have been lavished to provide guests with luxurious comfort and an extensive range of amenities.

The château was built in 1840 as the summer residence of the Boisgelin family, who had been associated with the area for over eight hundred years. Situated close to the coast, it shares a wooded park of over 200 hundred acres with the granite manor-house built in the sixteenth and seventeenth centuries that is today the home of the château's proprietor, the Marquis de Boisgelin.

During the Second World War, the château was occupied by the Germans and afterwards left abandoned. In 1980 it was reconstructed and restored. Now it is a hotel of high quality. Everywhere has been exquisitely decorated with a harmonising blend of colours, fabric and furniture. There are expensive rugs on the highly polished floors; wood panelling in some of the bedrooms; and chandeliers in almost every room. Even when the furnishings are unashamedly modern - as they are in the circular bar - they perfectly match the general ambience. All the bedrooms are both spacious and delightful, but, for even greater luxury, book the bridal suite in the circular tower.

So many facilities are provided for guests that they need never leave the grounds. Not only is there golf, horse-riding, fishing, tennis and a swimming-pool (unheated), but there are also facilities for children, including a playroom and table-tennis.

The modern Breton cooking of the chef, M. Louis Le Roy, is rightly renowned. The desserts are especially good. For an extra charge, guests can take his gourmet cookery course. First, they accompany him to market and then, in the château's kitchen, they study both nouvelle and traditional cuisine during a 3-hour demonstration. Finally, at lunch, they eat the dishes that they have helped to prepare.

There are two golf courses close-by, for those who want a greater challenge than is provided by the château's 9-hole fun-course. Both the St Samson Golf Course and Les Ajoncs d'Or Golf Course at Etables-sur-Mer are par 72 and situated in beautiful countryside.

The efficient and most helpful staff will make arrangements for guests who want to use these golf courses, as well as those who wish to go sailing, wind-surfing or sea-fishing. For those who look for peace and seclusion, there are many walks that can be taken through the château's extensive grounds.

Château Hôtel de Coatguelen is an ideal place for a prolonged stay. Because of the many amenities provided and the hotel's high reputation, the guests cover a wide age-range. It is usual to find most agreeable company there. The warm welcome is guaranteed.

POMMERIT-JAUDY - La Roche-Derrien BRITTANY - Côtes-du-Nord

24 CHATEAU DE KERMEZEN PG

♛♛★★
Pommerit-Jaudy, 22450 La Roche-Derrien, Côtes-du-Nord.
Tel: 96 91 35 75
Propr: Comte and Comtesse Michel de Kermel
Open: 1 Mar - 30 Nov

Twin with bath	2 B
Double with bath	2 B
Suite (max. 4)	1 C
Total rooms:	5
No lift	
Table d'hôte (res. only)	A
Dinner only: 20.30	

Groups: max. 8
No credit cards
English spoken
Tennis court 2km
Horse riding 20km
Golf course 30km
Sea 14km

Château Accueil
Les Etapes Francois Coeur

23km north of Guingamp. From there, take the D8 towards La Roche-Derrien. After 21km, at Pommerit-Jaudy, turn left on to an unmarked road, which leads to Kermezen. At a T-junction, with the church in front, turn to the left. The château is on the right. **Airport:** *Lannion (20km)* **Station:** *Guingamp (23km)*

Members of the old French aristocracy are often charming and delightful hosts with a fund of stories to tell about their home, ancestors and locality. Comte and Comtesse de Kermel are such a couple. They wish to welcome guests into their splendid home as friends and to make their stay memorable.

Château de Kermezen has been in their family for over five hundred years. The present building was constructed in the seventeenth century in the typical Breton style. Managing to look both sturdy and comfortable, it has a square tower at the front, while at the back there is both a square and a round tower. In the front of the roof, there are pretty ornamented dormer windows. The interior is charming - full of old and antique furniture. A great deal of trouble has been taken over the guest bedrooms, which have matching patterns on walls, curtains, bedspread and even upholstery. This might sound a trifle intrusive, but it is prettily done and as there is beautiful furniture in all the rooms - and in some there are old polished floorboards - the overall effect is impressive. The grounds of twelve acres, overlooking a small river, are most attractive, especially at the back of the house where flower-beds cluster close to the old granite walls. The place is peaceful, the atmosphere is homely, and the hosts are charming. Strongly recommended.

Chateau de Kermezen (24) Côtes-du-Nord (Brittany)

25 CHATEAU DE KERAMBLEIZ H

★★
Plomelin, 29000 Quimper, Finistère.
Tel: 98 94 23 42, 98 95 64 01
Propr: S.A.B.
Direc: M. B. Alterio
Open: Easter - 30 Sep

No lift. 2 ground-floor rooms.

Twin with shower	2	B
Double with shower	5	B-C
Double with bath	4	C
Suite (max. 4)	1	D
Total rooms:	12	

Apartments: 8 (in a converted annexe)

No restaurant

Seminars: max. 30
Groups: max. 40

Credit cards:
Diners Club
Eurocard, Visa
English, German & Italian spoken

Swimming pool
Tennis courts 2km
Horse riding 4km
Close to sea

Châteaux Hôtels Indép.

8km south-west of Quimper. From there, take the D785 towards Pont-l'Abbé, but after 2km, towards the end of the built-up area, turn left on to the D20. The château is on the left after 6km. **Airport:** *Quimper (8km)* **Station:** *Quimper (8km)*

Although, from the distance, it looks as though it might be older and more interesting, this is a late nineteenth-century château that was entirely renovated in 1985. The public rooms, with their parquet floors and wood panelling, have been well furnished and decorated in a style befitting the period. There are paintings on the walls, fresh flowers on the tables and pleasant rugs on the floor.

In contrast, the apartments in the converted annex are very modern, with white walls and pine furniture. The most delightful thing about the château is its position, overlooking the River Odet. A grassy meadow runs down to the water's edge, which is overhung with oak and pine trees. A small muddy bank offers mooring for dingies and a peaceful haven for anglers. At the back of the château there is a small swimming pool and there are many delightful walks through the 45-acre estate. It is a very pleasant spot, close to the coast. The hotel is run by a friendly and efficient staff.

PONT-L'ABBE BRITTANY - Finistère

26 CHATEAU DE KERNUZ H

♛♛♛ ★★
Route de Penmarc'h, 29120
Pont-l'Abbé, Finistère.
Tel: 98 87 01 59
Propr: M. Maufras du Châtellier
Open: 1 Apr - 30 Sep

Twin with shower	1 B
Twin with bath	7 B
Double with shower	1 B
Double with bath	2 B
Suite (max. 5)	1 C
Total rooms:	12

Restaurant: Open daily
Lunch: 1200 - 1300
Dinner: 1930 - 2000
Prix fixe: 1 menu at A
A la carte available
Demi-pension (2 days+) B
Specialities: *Filet de Julienne crème d'oseille; Lotte braisée au cidre; Fruits de mer; Cuisine saisonnière tradtionnelle.*

No lift.

Seminars: max. 30
Groups: max. 20
Receptions: max. 100
Credit cards:
Access, Eurocard
Mastercard, Visa
English spoken

Swimming pool
Close to sea
Tennis court 2km
Golf course 10km

Châteaux Hôtels Indép.

23km south-west of Quimper. From there, take the D785 to Pont-l'Abbé. Continue on the D785, towards Penmarc'h, but after 2.5km turn left on to the narrow road that leads to the château. **Airport:** *Quimper (20km)* **Station:** *Quimper (23km)*

The discovery within the walled grounds of ancient weapons and medallions supports the theory that the original Château de Kernuz was first a military fortification during the fourteenth century. The original building was destroyed by fire and the one that stands today was constructed in the sixteenth century. It is a starkly imposing château with an enormously long, grey-stone facade and two large towers. The gardens are fascinating, with shaded walks, immaculate lawns, old moss-covered oaks, and gnarled apple trees.

Although the exterior of the château may seem somewhat sombre, it is the hospitality and kindness of the owners that give Kernuz its special appeal.

The public rooms are charming and intimate, furnished with an interesting mixture of paintings, secretaires, amrchairs and chests that have been in the family for generations. Though comfortable, the bedrooms are not luxurious and some of the bathrooms are best described as being frugal. The food is traditional, wholesome and exceptionally cheap.

This is a château of great character and spirit. Strongly recommended.

IRODOUER BRITTANY - Ille-et-Vilaine

27 CHATEAU DU QUENGO PG

♥♥♥ ♀
35850 Irodouer, Ille-et Vilaine.
Tel: 99 39 81 47
Propr: Vicomte and Vicomtesse du Crest de Lorgerie
Open: All the year

No lift

Twin with bidet	2 A
Double with bidet	1 A
Double	1 A
Single	1 A
Total rooms:	5

(All rooms have a wash-basin, but all five rooms share two w.c.s and one bathroom.)

No restaurant

Groups: max. 10
No credit cards
English & German spoken

Riding
Fishing
Tennis 3km

Gîtes de France

32km north-west of Rennes. From there, take the N12-E50 towards Saint Brieuc. After 22km, turn off on to the D70 towards Bécherel. After 7.5km, immediately on entering Irodouer, turn right on to the D21 towards Romillé. The entrance to the château is a further 2km, on the left. **Airport:** *Rennes (30km)* **Station:** *Montauban de Bretagne (12km)*

Irodouer is hard to pronounce; the château's even harder to find. If you blink, you miss it. An ancient 'Gite' sign on a gate-post at the edge of the road is the only hint of the château's existence. After 500 m the fir-lined drive eventually passes through a dilapidated, arched gateway and, across a vast grassy expanse, stands Château du Quengo, grey and imposing. The drive circles round the rough-cut lawn, passing a tiny, ancient family chapel, before arriving at the flight of steps leading up to the château. Parthenosis quinquefolia creeps hungrily over the grey, granite walls and softens their austerity.

The entrance hall is simple but splendid. Ancient, patterned tiles cover the floors and in one corner a well-preserved sedan chair casually sits out its retirement. The high stone walls are clad with thick, brown, herring-bone twill, on which are still visible the faint traces of a gold fleur-de-lis pattern that once covered it. A wide flight of stone steps sweeps round and up to the first floor. On the wall above hangs an enormous portrait of an early Duke of Saxony, whom the du Crest family served until they left for Brittany in 1220.

Upstairs, the polished oak floor gently undulates. Our spacious room had a high, comfortable bed set back in an alcove and pleasant old furniture, but it was somewhat spoiled by giant sunflower wallpaper that seemed out of place. Partitioned off in one corner was a wash-basin and an unnervingly mobile, space-saving bidet. Next to this bedroom is the communal bathroom, with a huge bath and a polite notice warning that the hot water will take a long time to come through. The nearest toilet is along the sloping corridor. Torches are thoughtfully provided in each room so that it's easier in the dark to find the elusive light-switches.

Downstairs, the guests have a large sitting-room and dining room. Both are furnished with beautiful antiques, chandeliers and ornate mirrors. In an ante-room is a vast, intricately carved chest that was made by Spanish prisoners captured by Breton pirates in the seventeenth century. The beautiful, old oak floors are highly polished and seem no longer used to trampling feet. The whole house has the atmosphere of a grand family home that after years of bustle has sunk gratefully into a tranquil slumber.

The kitchen, with its comfortable chairs and clutter is obviously the most used room in the château. We chose to have our breakfast there with the Vicomte and Vicomtesse who are wonderfully hospitable and have many fascinating tales to tell about their home, of which they are justifiably proud.

The original house was built in the middle of the fifteenth century, but much of it was destroyed during the religious wars. All that now remains from that period is a lodge with two circular windows. The present château was built at the end of the sixteenth century with giant blocks of granite - the exterior walls are over three feet thick. At the beginning of the French Revolution, the château was a headquarters of the Royalists. In August, 1793, Republican soldiers attacked and four Royalists were shot in front of the château. In May 1793, the château was ransacked and badly damaged by Republicans. In 1822, after the Restoration, Château du Quengo was renovated, although the only change made to the exterior of the building was that the original windows were considerably enlarged.

The father of the present Vicomte was determined that history would not repeat itself when the Second World War broke out. All the furniture that is now in the house was loaded on to carts and taken away to be hidden in distant lofts and barns. In August 1940, a German lieutenant arrived at the château with a troop of soldiers. He demanded to be taken down into the wine cellars. The keys were produced, the vast door creaked open and the officer slapped his thigh with delight as he saw rack upon rack of wine bottles. He rushed forward, picked out a bottle and then threw it to the floor. He did this several times before he realised that every bottle was empty. In the nine months following the outbreak of war, the old Vicomte and his wife had drunk the entire contents of the wine-cellar that his family had accumulated for the best part of a century.

The present Vicomte has many more such stories to tell - of his family, of his château, and of his career after the war as a cavalry officer in North Africa. Both he and his wife genuinely love having guests - including children - in their home. Staying with them is a delightful experience.

JANZE BRITTANY - Ille-et-Vilaine

28 CHATEAU LA FRANCEULE PG

35150 Janzé, Ille-et-Vilaine.
Tel: 99 44 47 45
Propr: Mme Briand
Open: 1 Mar - 30 Oct

Double 4 A
(All bedrooms are on the second floor and share a bathroom and w.c.)

No lift
Table d'hôte on reservation
No credit cards

25km south-east of Rennes. From there, take the D163 towards Châteaubriant. After 13km, turn left on the D41 to Janzé. In the town, turn left on to the D777 towards Vitré. 4km later, after passing through Néron, take the first right when you see a sign for La Franceule. The narrow country lane crosses a bridge and then another sign points sharp right through a farm-yard. On the left, take a drive that passes through a flourishing orchard and eventually reaches the château. **Airport:** *Rennes (22km)* **Station:** *Janzé (2km)*

This somewhat weather-beaten château was built in the nineteenth century with red brick and ornamented with white stone. There are wrought-iron balconies and wooden shutters at each window. A double flight of stone steps sweeps up to the once grand entrance.

Grass sprouts from the gravel drive and weeds have overrun the central flower bed. Peacocks and turkeys wander round the garden and sheep graze happily in the long grass at the back of the château.

Inside is rather austere, with dark brown paint, oak floor boards and a wide uncarpeted staircase. At the top of this, there is another, narrower flight of stairs that leads to the guest rooms on the second floor. All are newly decorated in a simple, country style. There are rugs on the polished floors and huge old-fashioned china wash-basins in each room. A sombre atmosphere pervades much of the house, but the couple of bedrooms at the rear of the château overlook the spectacular valley and are light and pleasant. The communal bathroom is new and immaculate.

29 CHATEAU DE LEAUVILLE PG

⛉⛉ ★★
Landujan, 35360
Montauban-de-Bretagne,
Ille-et-Vilaine
Tel: 99 07 21 14
Propr: Mme Marie-Pierre & M. Patrick Gicquiaux
Open: All the year (reservations only in winter)

Table d'hôte (res. only) A
Dinner: 2000
Demi-pension B
Specialities: *Cuisine traditionnelle saisonnière; Brochette de lotte au beurre blanc et sauce corail; Terrine de saumon fumé et crème acidulée*

Credit cards:
Access,
Mastercard, Visa
English spoken

Swimming pool
Tennis courts 7km
Horse riding 15km
Golf course 30km

Twin with bath	4 B
Double with bath	2 C
Total rooms: 6	

Seminars: max. 20
Groups: max. 12
Receptions: max. 80

Châteaux Hôtels Indép.
Château Accueil
Les Etapes Francois Coeur
Gîtes de France

No lift

28km south of Dinan. From there, take the D2 to Bécherel, where turn right on to the D20 and pass through the centre of the old town. Shortly afterwards, there is a left turn on the D70 to Montfort. Do not take this, but take the next left on to the D71 towards Montauban. Château de Léauville is on the left, 6km further on and 1km before Landujan. **Airport:** *Rennes (35km)* **Station:** *Montauban (8km) or Rennes*

Château de Léauville is set in a beautiful, verdant and peaceful landscape. As we drove slowly up the long, tree-lined drive, sheep with their lambs ambled casually out of our way.

The squat, tiny château looks almost like a toy castle. Part of its garden is walled; the rest is separated from the neighbouring meadows by an ancient moat. At one corner there is a round tower with a cupola on top of the slated dome. At the other end of the facade is a small chapel. Protruding from the roof is a giant, central chimney. Small pink roses ramble over the yellow stone walls; pansies and marigolds cluster round the open front door.

The entrance hall is tiny. From there, a circular stone staircase leads to the bedrooms. Beyond is the central room of the château, with its beamed ceiling and enormous open fire-place, around which comfortable chairs are arranged. But dominating the whole room is a massive refectory table where guests have breakfast and dinner.

For many people, the evening meal is a highpoint of their stay at Léauville. Marie-Pierre is an excellent hostess, who speaks very good English. She and her husband manage to create an informal dinner party atmosphere which brings out the best in all their guests so that most evenings are full of laughter and conversation. The food is splendid and the menu changes every night. Good local wine is included in the cost.

The bedrooms are charming, with crocheted rugs on polished wooden floors, pretty bedside lamps and cheerful curtains and bedcovers. Outside, there is a flower garden and ancient yew trees. At the back of the château is a new swimming-pool with a paved sunbathing area and wonderfully comfortable sun-loungers.

The young and charming owners do everything they can to make their guests feel at home. They have thoughtfully and sympathetically restored a château that was built in the seventeenth century on the site of - and still contains some features of - an eleventh century manor house. It is a beautiful home in a tranquil, rural setting.

PLEUGUENEUC - St-Pierre-de-Plesguen BRITTANY - Ille-et-Vilaine

30 CHATEAU DE LA MOTTE BEAUMANOIR PG

♥♥ ★★
35720 Pleugueneuc (St-Pierre-de-Plesguen), Ille-et Vilaine.
Tel: 99 69 46 01
Propr: M. Charles and Mme Jacqueline Bernard
Direc: M. Eric Bernard
Open: All year

No lift

Twin with bath	2	C
Double with bath	4	C
Suites (max. 4)	2	D
Total rooms:	8	

Table d'hôte (res. only) A

Seminars: max. 25
Groups: max. 8
Credit cards:
Diners Club
Visa

English spoken

Tennis court 3km
Horse riding 5km
Swimming pool 12km
Golf 12km, 15km

Châteaux Hôtels Indép.
Château Accueil

Gîtes de France

12km south-east of Dinan. From there, take the D794 eastwards towards Combourg. After 10km, turn right on to the D79 to Plesder. There turn left on to the D78. The château is on the right after 750m. **Airport:** *Dinan (12km)* **Station:** *Dinan or Combourg (14km)*

Passing through a small copse and a farmyard, the tree-lined drive leads into the gravelled courtyard of this impressive, grey-granite château. In front is the proprietor's private wing and to the left is the old stable-block. To the right is the massive main building, where the guests are accommodated. This three-storeyed section dates from the mid-eighteenth century, when the property was owned by the Beaumanoir family, but other parts of the château were constructed in the fifteenth century on the foundations of a feudal keep. After the French Revolution, the château was acquired by the de Lorgerils, who built up substantial land-holdings in the area. The family still lives nearby in the Château de la Bourbansais. In the years after the Second World War, La Motte Beaumanoir stood empty and fell into decay.

That the Bernard family has had to undertake much restoration work since it acquired the château is obvious as soon as you walk through the door. Everywhere is pristine, though retaining much of the atmosphere of an ancient building. Stone floors smooth with age, giant oak beams, and fireplaces large enough to roast an ox are successfully blended with comfortable modern furniture in the lounge and dining room.

Upstairs, the bedrooms are stylish, with sparkling white-cotton macramé bedspreads, attractive furniture and curtains. Each room has its own character. The most recently completed is a delightful honeymoon suite at the top of the tower - it has a four-poster bed and absolute privacy. Outside, there is a terrace overlooking an enormous lake that was created a few years ago in what had been a boggy meadow.

Charles and Jacqueline Bernard work successfully with their children, Eric and Isabelle, to provide a welcoming, family atmosphere and considerable comfort for their guests.

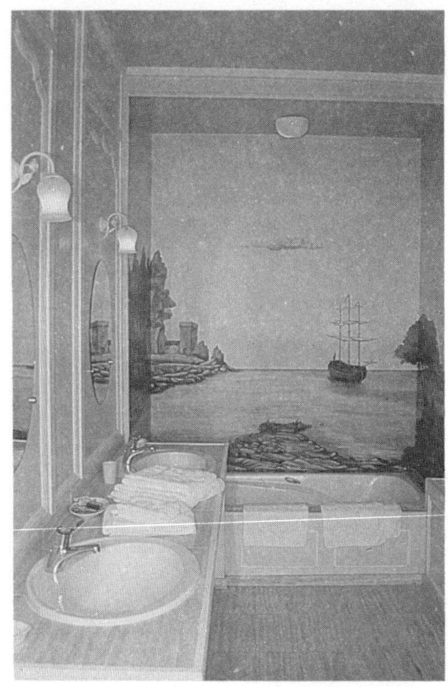

31 CHATEAU DES BLOSSES PG

♥♥★★
35460 Saint-Ouen-la-Rouerie, Ille-et-Vilaine.
Tel: 99 98 36 16
Propr: M. and Mme Jacques Barbier
Open: 11 Feb -14 Nov

Twin with bath	3 B-C
Double with bath (inc. breakfast)	2 B-C
Total rooms:	5

No lift

Table d'hôte on reservation:
Ordinaire at A
Special Tradition Francais, including Champagne at B
Chef: Mme Barbier
Dinner only: 2000

Groups: max. 10

Credit cards: Visa
English spoken

Putting
Tennis courts 2km
Horse riding 12km
Sea 20km
Swimming pool 25km
Château Hôtels Indep.
Château Accueil
Gîtes de France

28km north-west of Fougères. From there, take the D155 towards Antrain. Just before reaching there, after 25km, turn right on the D296 to Saint-Ouen-la-Rouerie. The château is less than 1km further, on the left. **Airport:** *Rennes (46km)* **Station:** *Pontorson (11km)*

This is a typical nineteenth century château - a square, red-brick building with white-stone facings around the doors and windows. It is solid, fussy and rather ugly. But the interior is far more attractive and interesting. Its large, dingy-brown entrance-hall is filled with a mixture of the fascinating and the mundane. A beautiful old tapestry hangs opposite a row of muddy, wellington boots; stuffed animal heads peer down through the gloom. Half-way up the wide wooden staircase is a large stained-glass window - its brilliant blue glows as sunlight streams through. Upstairs is an enormous landing, with a strip of sisal matting running the length of the polished wooden floor. High glass-fronted bookcases, packed full with ancient leather-bound volumes stand against one wall. Opposite is a settee with delicately curved legs and an ancient metal cot. By the window is a large circular table on which stands an enormous vase full of wild flowers. Great care has been given to decorating and furnishing the large bedrooms with matching colours and fabrics, so that each room is interesting and pleasantly grand. Because the floors are highly polished wood, dotted with occasional rugs, some people might feel that the bedrooms seem slightly bare, but for the purist all is as it should be.

Downstairs, the sitting-room and dining room are large, bright and attractive - full of paintings, objets d'art and antique furniture in a variety of styles. All the windows look out on to the tranquil parkland and woods, which are a part of M. Barbier's 750-acre farm. He and his wife are entertaining company and their evening meals have the atmosphere of a dinner-party of friends. Nothing about their home is gimmicky - it has a lived-in, comfortable feel.

The estate originally belonged to the ancient family of La Rouerie. The last of their number was the Marquis Armand de la Rouerie, an adventurer who sailed to America in 1777 to join in the War of Independence. Known to his fellow soldiers as 'Colonel Armand', he fought valiantly and was presented with the Cross of Cincinnatus by General George Washington. On his return to France, Armand found the country in turmoil. He became the leader of a royalist faction called 'La Chouannerie', which is derived from 'chouette', the French word for an owl. This was because the Royalists used the cry of their owl at night as a signal and a battle cry. Armand was killed on a neighbouring estate in 1793.

In 1824, the Barbier family bought La Rouerie with its lands and the old château, in which M. Barbier's mother now lives. His great-grandfather built des Blosses between 1888 and 1890 as a home for his children. There, he hoped, new generations of the Barbier family would flourish and so he named the new château after the cherry-tree's white blooms - 'blosses'.

32 CHATEAU DE KERAVEON H

🛡 ★★
56410 Erdeven, Morbihan.
Tel: 97 55 68 55
Propr: M. Diamedo Jean-Paul Géraud
Open: 15 May - 15 Sep

Double with shower	1 D
Double with bath	15 D
Suites	4 F-G
Total rooms: 20	

Lift

Restaurant: Open daily
Chef: M. Gerard Jehanno
Prix fixe: Menus at A & B
A la carte available
Demi-pension (3 days +) - obligatory in season C

Credit cards:
Mastercard, Visa
English & German spoken

Swimming pool
Horse riding 500m
Tennis court 3km
Golf course 3km

Châteaux Hôtels Indép.

20km south-east of Hennebont. From there, take the D9. After 15km, the road meets the D781. Turn left and after crossing the River Etel, bear right, still on the D781. Erdeven is another 5km. In the village, opposite the church, turn left on to a small road. The château is a further 1.5km on the left. **Airport:** *Lorient (20km)* **Station:** *Auray (15km)*

It all sounds wonderful - an eighteenth-century château built on the foundations of a sixteenth-century castle, a moat, an ancient watch-tower, a Renaissance well, a stone keep, a pigeon house, and a swimming-pool. But not all expectations are fulfilled. Ivy creeps up the attractive facade, but the keep fits uneasily at the back of the building, looking a little like a bizarre water-tower or a Byzantine space-ship. Inside, the château has an old-fashioned air. Everywhere is immaculate, there are some nice pieces of furniture and care has been taken with the decorations; but some of the bedrooms are far too ornately-patterned for our taste. The dining room has carefully repointed granite-block walls and a large, impressive tapestry. All the bedrooms are spacious, as are the public rooms, which are attractively decorated and uncluttered. The service is good and the restaurant acceptable.

The surrounding area, especially the white sands of Erdeven Beach, is well worth a visit.

HENNEBONT BRITTANY- Morbihan

33 CHATEAU DE LOCGUENOLE H

⛉ ★★★
Route de Port-Louis, 56700 Hennebont, Morbihan.
Tel: 97 76 29 04
Telex: 950 636 F
Propr: Mme Alyette de la Sablière
Open: 1 Mar - 30 Nov

Twin with bath	10	B-E
Double with bath	25	B-E
Suites	2	D-H
Total rooms:	37	

(12 rooms in an annexe)

No lift. 10 ground-floor rooms.

Restaurant: Open daily
Chef: M. Michel Gaudin
Lunch: 1230 - 1400
Dinner: 1930 - 2130
Prix fixe: Menus at A & B
A la carte available
Demi-pension - obligatory in high season C-E
Specialities: *Persillé de ris de veau et langoustines; Lotte rôtie au lard fumé; Chaud froid de poires caramélisées.*

Seminars: 5 conference rooms
Groups: max. 60
Credit cards:
American Express
Diners Club
Eurocard
Mastercard, Visa
English & German spoken

Swimming pool
Tennis court
Horse riding 5km
Golf course 20km

Relais & Châteaux

4.5km south of Hennebont. From there, take the D781. The drive to the château is on the right (just before the turn-off on the left to Kervignac). **Airport:** *Lorient (17km)* **Station:** *Hennebont (5km)*

Locguénolé is like many other French châteaux on two counts - first, the present building was built at the beginning of the nineteenth century to replace one destroyed during the French Revolution, and second, the estate has several times passed through female descendants into other families. (Madame de la Sablière, the present formidable owner, is able to trace her forebears at Locguénolé back to 1480.) But in one important respect, this château is different from all others. It is the only châteaux-hotel in France with a restaurant that in 1987 was awarded two Michelin rosettes. (It also has from Gault Millau three red toques and 17 out of 20 points.) The chef, Michel Gaudin, is famed throughout France for his presentation of seafoods and fresh garden produce (poached oysters with spinach, smoked salmon with leeks). His desserts are excellent.

Eating is a serious business in France and good dishes take time to prepare. Many British and American people are used to faster food and service. So some have expressed disappointment at what they regard as being slow service and a frosty atmosphere. We did not find this to be so. Nor is the food expensive in comparison with other restaurants of this quality. We certainly paid far more elsewhere for meals that were nowhere near as good as those at Locquénolé.

On one wall of the gracious dining room is a priceless Aubusson tapestry. On the opposite side, the windows look out over the grassy meadow that slopes down to the gentle waters of the River Blavet, where fishing-boats chug to and fro. The vast grounds of nearly 250 acres contain dense woods of ancient trees and many pleasant walks. There is also a heated swimming pool and a tennis court.

The interior of this large, grey-stone château is impressive. There are oriental carpets on the polished parquet-floors and beautiful antiques in most of the rooms. It is true that there is a formal air about Locquénolé. It is true that staying there is not cheap. But it does have an individual style which with the peacefulness of its surroundings makes it an ideal retreat for those seeking seclusion and exclusivity.

34 DOMAINE DU CHATEAU DE ROCHEVILAINE H

★★★
Pointe de Pen-Lan, Billiers,
56190 Muzillac, Morbihan.
Tel: 97 41 69 27
Telex: 950 570 F
D. G.: M. Patrick Gasnier
Direc: Mme Josette Andrea Finck
Open: 21 Feb - 4 Jan
Twin with bath 14 B-E
Double with bath 13 B-E
Total rooms: 27
Apartment: 1 (max. 5)

Restaurant: Open daily
Chef: M. Patrice Caillaut
Lunch: 1230 - 1330
Dinner: 1930 - 2100
Prix fixe: 2 menus at B
A la carte available
Demi-pension (4 days+) D
Specialities: *Homard rôti au beurre de corail; Ravioles d'huîtres dans leur jus.*

No lift. 8 ground-floor rooms.

Seminars: max. 30
Credit cards:
Access
American Express
Diners Card
Mastercard
Visa
English & German spoken
Swimming pool
By the sea
Tennis courts 300m
Horse riding 1.5km
Golf course 30km

27km south-east of Vannes. From there, take the N165 and exit at Muzillac. From there, take the D5 south to Pointe de Pen-Lan. Le Rochevilaine is at the end of the road. **Airport:** *Nantes (75km)* **Station:** *Vannes (18km)*

The granite buildings of the Domaine du Château de Rochevilaine form a small village perched on a rocky promontory above the sea. It is a unique and special place, washed by the Gulf Stream, where the sun shines for over 2,000 hrs a year.

Between the road and the hotel there is a tree-shaded garden, but the buildings face the sea. In the rocks below there is a delightful swimming pool and a sea-water pond containing freshly-caught lobsters and langoustines.

The oak-floored, public rooms have large windows overlooking the sea. The lounge has a giant stone fireplace and among the brocade-upholstered arm-chairs are two ancient canons. The bedrooms, which are priced according to their size, are comfortable, although furnished and decorated without flair.

A special feature of the hotel is the traditional Breton cuisine and sea-food specialities of the chef, Patrice Caillaut. Wines from the Loire and Bordeaux feature strongly in the list, which includes, for any passing pools-winner, the 1976 Château Mouton Rothschild.

Top: **Château d'Audrieu** (1) Calvados (Normandy)
Bottom: **Château de la Roque** (15) Manche (Normandy)

Top: **Castel Marie-Louise** (36) Loire-Atlantique (Pays de la Loire)
Bottom: **Château des Reaux** (68) Indre-et-Loire (Centre)

35 HOSTELLERIE DE LA FERRIERE H

★
Route de Nantes, 44110 Châteaubriant, Loire-Atlantique.
Tel: 40 28 00 28
Telex: 701 353 F
Propr: M. René Duboc
Open: All year

Twin with bath	10 B
Double with bath	15 B
Total rooms:	25

No lift. 14 ground-floor rooms.

Restaurant: Open daily
Chef: M. Hubert
Lunch: 1215 - 1400
Dinner: 1930 - 2100
Prix fixe 2 menus at A
A la carte available
Demi-pension (3 days+) B
Specialities: *Cuisine bretonne; Assiette Nordique; Poisson beurre blanc; Tournedos aux cepes; Patisserie maison.*

Seminars: max. 30
Groups: max. 10
Receptions: max. 200
Credit cards:
American Express
Diners Card
Eurocard
Visa
English spoken

Châteaux Hôtels Indép.
Minotels France Accueil

The hotel is just outside Châteaubriant, on the left of the D178 to Nantes. **Airport:** *Nantes (75km)* **Station:** *Nantes (70km)*

Seen from the road, Château de la Ferrière has a romantic air, with its tall round spike-topped towers flanking each corner, its ivy-clad walls, the white shuttered windows, and complexly shaped roof. The original château was built in 1750 for M. Dublin de la Ferrière, but it was destroyed during the French Revolution. Rebuilt in 1830, it was occupied by a succession of rich families. Since 1973, it has been a hotel and now has few pretensions to grandeur. It is an efficient, pleasant hotel that is much used by tourists en route to somewhere else and by businessmen for seminars.

The staff are most helpful. The bedrooms are of a reasonable size and unassuming. Some have been redecorated in a sombre, dark green. The dining room is attractive and the food, though ambitious, is inexpensive. The gardens are well maintained. An ornamental lake, surrounded by trees, is crossed by a small wooden bridge.

LA BAULE PAYS DE LA LOIRE - Loire-Atlantique

36 CASTEL MARIE-LOUISE H

★★★

1 Avenue Andrieu, 44500
La Baule, Loire-Atlantique.
Tel: 40 60 20 60
Telex: 700 408 F
Propr: M. Lucien Barrière
Direc: M. David Lawton
Open: All year

Twin with bath	12 C-F
Double with bath	18 C-F
Suites	2 F-I
Total rooms:	32

Lift. 2 rooms equipped for the handicapped. 6 rooms on ground floor.

Restaurant: Open daily
Chef: M. Eric Mignard
Lunch: 1230 - 1400
Dinner: 1930 - 22.00
Prix fixe: Menus at A & B
A la carte available
Demi-pension (2 days+) - cost of room + B
Specialities: *Marinière de homard flambée au pur malt et cassolette de riz sauvage; Confit de turbot aux pleurotes et ris de veau parfumé aux salpicons de gingembre.*

Seminars: max. 20
Groups: max. 15
Credit cards:
American Express
Diners Club
Visa
English & Spanish spoken

Swimming pool 100m
Tennis courts 400m
Close to sea
Windsurfing
Golf course 6km

Relais & Châteaux

On the Atlantic coast, 16km west of Saint Nazaire. From there, take the D92 and in La Baule keep to the sea-front. Leave the main esplanade at the Casino. Take the first left into Avenue des Lilas. Castel Marie-Louise is at the next junction on the left. **Airport:** *Saint Nazaire (15km)* **Station:** *La Baule-Esoublac*

La Baule is one of the most popular seaside resorts in northern France and it claims to have the most beautiful beach in Europe. More justifiably, Castel Marie-Louise claims to have the finest cuisine in the area. Michelin has rightly awarded the restaurant a rosette for the cuisine gastronomique traditionnelle of the young chef, Eric Mignard. Naturally, the menus concentrate on sea food, and the presentation and innovative touches are delightful. So is the restaurant, with its soft beige colouring and large windows looking out across the garden to the sea.

The colour-schemes used to decorate all the rooms have been well chosen. The bedrooms are attractive and the bathrooms excellent. Guests are able to use the heated sea-water swimming pool in the nearby Hotel Hermitage.

Built in 1905, the Castel Marie-Louise has been a hotel since 1926. The refurbishment in 1986 has ensured that its high standards are maintained.

BLAISON - Brissac-Quincé PAYS DE LA LOIRE - Maine-et-Loire

37 CHATEAU DE CHEMAN PG

♛♛ ★	Double with shower 1 B	No credit cards
Blaison, 49320 Brissac-Quincé, Maine-et-Loire.	Double with bath 1 B (inc. breakfast)	Tennis court 1km
Tel: 41 57 17 60	Total rooms: 2	Swimming pool 9km
Propr: Mme Alvina Antoine		
Open: All year	No restaurant	Gîtes de France

On the south bank of the Loire, 11km south-east of Angers. Blaison can be reached by many small, winding roads, but from Angers the easiest way is to take the D952 east along the north bank of the Loire. At Saint-Mathurin-sur-Loire (the first crossing-point) turn right over the bridge. Immediately afterwards, turn right on to the D132 to Blaison. The château is a little further along on the left. **Airport:** *Angers (13km)* **Station:** *Angers (11km)*

This ancient château is at the heart of a working vineyard that from its Cabernet grapes produces fine red and rosé wines. The rendered-stone buildings clustered round a large courtyard include the house, storerooms and a deconsecrated chapel in which earlier owners of the château were buried. The oldest part now remaining is a slender circular tower dating from the sixteenth century. Much of the rest was added a hundred years later. Like most châteaux in the area, Cheman was originally owned by a rich and powerful family who were deprived of their property at the time of the French Revolution.

Although the exterior has a pleasant, decaying appearance, the interior has been well maintained. In the dining room, there are thick, black beams on the ceiling and terracotta tiles on the floor. The great stone fireplace is decorated with old weapons and pieces of armour. In the large bedrooms there are rugs on the polished wooden floors and attractive period furniture.

It is an ideal place to stay for those wishing to experience life in the French countryside.

38 CHATEAU DES BRIOTTIERES PG

♁♁♁ ★★♈
49330 Champigné, Maine-et-Loire.
Tel: 41 42 00 02
Telex: 720 943 F
Propr: M. Francois & Mme Hedwige de Valbray
Open: 15 Feb - 15 Dec

Twin with bath	3 C
Double with bath	3 C
Suites	2 D
Twin rooms	1 D
Total rooms:	9

Apartments: 1

Table d'hôte on request B (inc. wine)
Dinner: 2000
Demi-pension C
Specialities: *Pains de champignons, Veau orloff; terrine de poisson; Brochet au beurre blanc; Saumon a l'oseille; Parfait aux frambois.*

Seminars: max. 15
Groups: max. 15
Receptions: max. 300

Credit cards:
Am Ex, Diners Club
Eurocard, Visa
English & Spanish spoken

Fishing
Swimming pool 3km
Tennis court 3km
Golf 20km

Châteaux Hôtels Indép.
Château Accueil
Inter. Leading Association
Les Etapes Francois Coeur

33km north of Angers. From there, take the D107 north to Feneu, where at the junction with the D768 turn right. Continue to Champigné, where the road crosses over the D770. Continue through Champigné, but then take the first left (D190). After 2km, and just after a road on the left to Querré, is the drive to the château. **Airport:** *Angers (30km)* **Station:** *Cable (25km)*

Set in a park of over 200 acres, this impressive château was built in 1760 above extensive wine cellars dating from the fifteenth century. Beautifully proportioned, with a small wing at either end of the long central section, the château's many windows look out over an idyllic rural landscape. In 1850 a single-floored gallery was built in front of the centre of the house, but this in no way spoils the building's elegant design. It forms a vast entrance hall in which the floor-to-ceiling windows and thriving plants create a bright and welcoming atmosphere.

The spacious and grand rooms off the gallery are furnished with beautiful antiques and paintings, many of which have been in the de Valbray family for six generations. Despite these priceless treasures, there is a well-worn feel about the château that makes it obvious that it is a real family home. This and the friendliness of the enthusiastic young hosts, Francois and Hedwige de Valbray, ensure that guests are able to relax in the impressive, authentic surroundings.

The bedrooms are comfortable and pleasantly decorated in various styles. Each is given a descriptive name, including 'Rose', 'Jaune Empire' and, for one of the simpler rooms, 'Cloche'. The bathrooms are immaculate and well-equipped.

Meals are served at an enormous D-ended dining-table, where guests eat *en famille.* The dinner is cooked by Mme de Valbray and is a splendid, sociable occasion. There is a fixed menu, which changes daily, and the price includes coffee and the family's own pleasant wine.

During the summer months, several special events are arranged in the grounds of the château. There are concerts and plays. On the third Sunday in July there is a Medieval Fete in which 250 people in costumes participate.

In the past, many famous people stayed in the château, including the author Madame de Stael. The tradition continues. Its informal elegance and style have made the château very popular. (Bookings during Le Mans week need to be made six months in advance.) Staying at Les Briottières is a genuine opportunity to experience the authentic 'vie de château'.

CHEFFES-SUR-SARTHE - Tiercé PAYS DE LA LOIRE - Maine-et-Loire

39 CHATEAU DE TEILDRAS H

⛉⛉ ★★★
Cheffes-sur-Sarthe, 49125
Tiercé, Maine-et-Loire
Tel: 41 42 61 08
Telex: 722 268 F
Propr: Comte de Bernard du Breuil
Open: All year

Twin with bath	7	D-E
Double with bath	4	E
Total rooms:	11	

No lift

Restaurant: Closed for Tue lunch
Chef: M. Patrick Duqesnay
Lunch: 1230 - 1400
Dinner: 1930 - 2100
Prix fixe: 1 menu at B
A la carte available
Demi-pension D

Seminars: max. 25
Groups: max. 11
Credit cards:
American Express
Diners Club, Visa
English spoken

Fishing 500m
Tennis court 200m
Golf course 38km

Relais & Châteaux

25km north of Angers. From there, take the N23 north-east towards la Flèche, but after 4km turn left on to the D52 to Tiercé. There turn left on to the D74 to Cheffes-sur-Sarthe. The château is on a road to the right and is well sign-posted. **Airport:** *Angers (23km)* **Station:** *Angers (25km)*

This small, sixteenth-century château overlooks a lake and rolling fields. Ivy climbs up its white-stone walls to the grey-slated roof. Well proportioned, it has a square tower at the front and two small wings at the back. Enclosed by this is a beautiful terrace, where the air is filled with the fragrance of the many rose bushes that are Comte de Bernard du Breuil's all-absorbing passion. In the flower-beds there are lilies, geraniums and lavender - all helping to create the delightful setting.

There is an air of graciousness about the public rooms. Several, including a reception area and dining room, have beamed ceilings. Huge tapestries, gilt mirrors and paintings hang on the plain, coloured walls. The antique furniture is carefully arranged and on the shelves there are clusters of suitable bric-a-brac.

The bedrooms are also tastefully decorated. Some have beams, most have beautiful views of the 50-acre park, and all are luxurious. So are the bathrooms.

We have spoken to people who were delighted by everything at de Teildras. We found the atmosphere business-like. It is family-run, but it is a hotel first-and-foremost.

ECHEMIRE - Baugé PAYS DE LA LOIRE - Maine-et-Loire

40 CHATEAU DE LA GRIFFERAIE PG

★★

Echemiré, 49150 Baugé, Maine-et-Loire.
Tel: 41 89 70 25
Propr: M. J-M. Tixier
Open: Easter to 3 Nov

Twin with shower	2 B-C
Twin with bath	3 D
Double with shower	1 C
Double with bath	1 D
Suites (max. 4)	2 C-D
Total rooms:	9

No lift

Table d'hôte on reservation: 1 menu at A, 1 at B
Dinner only: 20.30
Specialities: *Foie gras de canard; Confrits; Magret de canard; Saumon et brochet de Loire beurre blanc; Production artisanale au château.*

Seminars: max. 35
Groups: max. 15
Credit cards: American Express, Visa
English spoken

Tennis court
Swimming pool 4km
Horse riding 6km
Golf course 30km

Châteaux Hôtels Indép.

35km north east of Angers. From there, take the N23 towards Durtal. After 20km, at Seiches-sur-le-Loir, turn right on to the D766. The château is 15km further on the right, just after the village of Echemiré. **Airport:** *Angers (38km)* **Station:** *Baugé (4km) or Angers*

La Grifferaie was built in the style of Louis XIII on the site of a seventeenth-century château. Completed in 1860, it is a white wedding-cake of a château, ornately layered and decorated wherever possible with fine stone carvings. The grey-slate roof is an assortment of various shaped turrets and some elaborate, tall chimneys. At the back, there is large formal rose garden that leads to a wide flight of stone steps with stone balustrades covered with climbing roses. At the front, there is another sweep of stairs. It leads to the entrance hall, which has been exotically decorated with animal-skin rugs, giant elephants' tusks, and other assorted Africana. Unusually for a French château, there is nothing feminine about the interior, which has an almost ostentatious, no-expense-spared look about the decorations and furniture. The rich deep-pile carpets, valuable antiques and choice objets d'art make it feel like the palace of an oriental prince or an international playboy. Guests dine round a common table in the evenings, something which helps create the unique character of a stay at la Grifferaie. Certainly worth a visit.

GREZ-NEUVILLE PAYS DE LA LOIRE - Maine-et-Loire

41 CHATEAU DE LA BEUVRIERE PG

★

Grez-Neuville, 49220 Le Lion-d'Angers, Maine-et-Loire.
Tel: 41 95 21 42
Propr: M. Noel Vandenberghe-Lebbe
Open: Christmas holidays & 1 Mar - 31 Oct
No lift

Single - shared w.c.	2	A
Twin with shower	3	B
Twin with bath	1	B
Double with shower	7	B
Double with bath	4	B
Suite	1	B
Total rooms:	18	

Table d'hôte on reservation
2 menus at A
Dinner Only: 1900 - 2200

Groups: max. 24
No credit cards
English, German, Dutch & Spanish spoken
Gîtes de France

20km north-west of Angers. From there, take the N162. After 16km, and 2km after La Membrolle-sur-Longuenée, turn left towards Brain-sur-Longuenée. The entrance to the château is 4km further, at the corner of the second turn on the right. **Airport:** *Angers (17km)* **Station:** *Angers (20km)*

As you crunch up the drive, an enormous hound bays loudly and tries to leap from his tomb-like enclosure. Ahead, Château de la Beuvrière looms up, a vast white-stone fortress with square towers and round towers and ornamental turrets. Like many other châteaux, it was built at the beginning of the nineteenth century on the site of a much earlier castle. A wide flight of steps with curved stone balustrades leads to the impressive front entrance. Above are two small turrets, their machicolations perfectly sited to fend off unwanted visitors with boiling oil.

No such reception now greets new arrivals. Instead, there is a delightful welcome from M. and Mme Vanderberghe, a Belgian couple. One-time interior designers, they have indulged their taste for lace tablecloths, net curtains, candlelabras, antique bric-a-brac, and a mirror above one of the vast fireplaces which at the touch of a switch suddenly turns into a window. The rooms are enormous, especially the guests' lounge which has a neo-Gothic bar and a large button-back, draylon-velvet three-piece suite. A double flight of carpeted white stone stairs leads from the beamed hall to apparently numberless rooms, some of which are still being renovated. The bedroom furnishing can best be described as Gothic-Wagnerian, and everywhere is spotless. The château is surrounded by vast, beautiful grounds that include a lake covering 24 acres.

LA JAILLE-YVON - Chambellay PAYS DE LA LOIRE - Maine-et-Loire

42 CHATEAU DU PLESSIS PG

♛♛ ★★ ♈

La Jaille-Yvon, 49990 Chambellay, Maine-et-Loire.
Tel: 41 95 12 75
Telex: 720943 F
Propr: M. & Mme Paul Benoist
Open: 1 Apr - 15 Oct

Twin with bath	2 B
Double with bath	4 B
Total rooms:	6

No lift

Table d'hôte on request A (Anjou wine included)
Chef: Mme Benoist
Dinner: 21.00 - 21.30
Specialities: *Filet mignon sauce grand veneur; Brochet* (pike) *beurre blanc; Poissons sauce au sherry; Vacherin du Plessis.*

Seminars: max. 15
Groups: max. 12

Credit cards:
American Express
Diners Club
Mastercard
Visa
English & Spanish spoken

Tennis court
Ballooning on request
Fishing 800m
Horse riding 15km
Golf course 35km
Châteaux Accueil
Châteaux Hôtels Indép.
Les Etapes Francois Coeur

33km north of Angers. From there, take the N162 northwards to Lion d'Angers. Continue through the town and again pick up the N162. After 10km, turn right on the D189 to La Jaille-Yvon. At a junction just before the village, turn right on to the D187. The château is just up the hill on the right-hand side. **Airport:** *Nantes (110km)* **Station:** *Angers (33km)*

Set in beautiful and extensive grounds, this vine-covered château looks out over sweeping lawns shaded by giant trees. It was built as a hunting lodge at the beginning of the sixteenth century. Two hundred years later, Plessis was restored and two extensive wings were added. This amalgamation produced an idosyncratic building that has great character and charm.

As they arrive, guests are warmly welcomed by their hosts, M. and Mme Benoist, who are a friendly, entertaining couple. They became hoteliers when Paul Benoist decided to give up his job abroad so that he could spend more time in his home.

It is easy to understand his affection for the château in which his family has lived since the middle of the eighteenth century. The history of the house since then is intertwined with that of his ancestors. In 1793, when one of them was guillotined in Angers at the beginning of the French Revolution, the mob dragged the furnishings from the château and set fire to them in the courtyard. Only the refectory table in the kitchen was left behind. It was too big and heavy to be moved. The table has remained in the kitchen to this day.

Because they are so well-informed about the history of the château and the surrounding countryside, M. and Mme Benoist are able to help their guests enjoy their stay in an area that boasts of having more châteaux and historical monuments than any other department in France.

Their home is a most agreeable place. The bright, cheerful rooms are furnished with many antiques. Family portraits hang on the walls, a huge vase of flowers stands on the grand piano, and Turkish rugs cover the wooden floors. Through a round skylight above the central entrance-hall, sunshine pours down on to the circular, polished oak staircase that leads upstairs. The bedrooms are attractive and much care had been taken to ensure that they are comfortable. Like the rest of the château the bathrooms are beyond reproach.

Breakfast is taken in the kitchen *en famille,* but the evening meal is served with style in the dining room. The food is the best of home-cooking. There is an intimate, friendly atmosphere about the château which is relaxing and most agreeable.

43 CHATEAU DE MONTREUIL PG

♛♛	Twin with shower 1 B	Table d'hôte (res. only) A
Montreuil-sur-Loir, 49140 Seiches-sur-Loir, Maine-et-Loire.	Double 1 A (inc. breakfast)	No credit cards
	Total rooms: 2	English spoken
Tel: 41 76 21 03	(Bedrooms share a w.c.)	Fishing
Propr: M. Jacques & Mme Marie Bailliou	Apartment: 1 (max. 5)	Swimming pool 5km
		Tennis court 5km
Open: 1 Mar - 30 Nov	No lift	Gîtes de France

21km north-east of Angers. From there, take the N23. At Seiches-sur-Loir, turn left on to the D74. The château is on the right, just after passing through Montreuil-sur-Loir. **Airport:** *Angers (24km)* **Station:** *Angers (21km)*

This handsome château was built in 1849 for the architect, René Hodé, in the neo-Gothic style known as 'Troubadour'. It replaced a château built in the fifteenth century. Of this older building there remains a small chapel and a splendid, large dovecote. The Bailliou family purchased the estate as a farm in 1925.

Both Jacques and Marie Bailliou are friendly, welcoming hosts, who are very proud of their home, which is in a magnificent setting. It stands on an escarpment overlooking the River Loir at a point where there is a massive weir. Through the large windows in most of the rooms, including the vast entrance hall, it is possible to enjoy the spectacular panorama.

The spacious, wood-panelled sitting-room is dominated by an ornate wooden overmantle. The furniture is comfortable and guests are encouraged to make themselves at home. Double doors lead into what was once the old kitchen, but is now a very pleasant dining room. Marie Bailliou is a good cook and, being a farmer's wife, has access to plenty of fresh vegetables. Her table d'hôte is splendid value. (Be warned. Her husband makes a most potent pear liquer.)

A circular stone staircase leads to the large bedrooms which seem a little bare. The w.c. is along the landing and has an old fashioned flushing-system that must be treated firmly if it is to be persuaded to work.

This imposing château has a subdued atmosphere, as though recently abandoned by a large, noisy family. But it is very good value and the setting is superb.

44 CHATEAU DE CRAON PG

♛♛♛ ★	Double	2 C-D	English spoken
53400 Craon, Mayenne.	Single	3 B	
Tel: 43 06 11 02	(inc. breakfast)		Swimming pool
Propr: Comte & Comtesse de Guébriant	Total rooms:	5	Tennis court 1km
			Horse riding 20km
Open: 1 Jun - 10 Sep	No restaurant		Golf course 30km
No lift	No credit cards		Château Accueil

37km north-east of Châteaubriant. From there, take the N171 through Pouance to Craon. Do not take the by-pass, but drive across it into the centre of the town. The long drive to the château is straight ahead, to the left of the church. **Airport:** *Angers (52km)* **Station:** *Laval (30km) or Craon*

Standing on the crest of a hill overlooking the town, Château de Craon was built for the d'Armaille family between 1770 and 1775. The architect, Pommeryol from Toulouse, was inspired by the classical style and designed a spectacularly beautiful building of elegant proportions and delicate ornamentation. The interior has the fine wood panelling and furniture of the period. The bedrooms are authentic and delightful. The hosts are charming. The château is surrounded by a hundred acres of formal gardens and landscaped park. The additional buildings, added at the beginning of the nineteenth century, include stables, an orangery, an ice-house and laundry. An important historical monument, it is open to the public every afternoon in July and August. An exquisite place.

SAINT-OUENS-DES-VALLONS - Montsûrs PAYS DE LA LOIRE - Mayenne

45 CHATEAU DE LA ROCHE-PICHEMER PG

⛉⛉⛉ ★

Saint-Ouen-des-Vallons, 53150 Montsûrs, Mayenne.	Double and bath	2 C	English spoken
	Apartment 1		
Tel: 43 90 00 41	No lift		Tennis court
Propr: Comte & Comtesse d'Ozouville			Fishing
	No restaurant		Swimming pool 10km
Open: 1 Jul - 31 Aug			Golf course 25km
(by reservation in June & September)	No credit cards		
			Château Accueil

24km north-east of Laval (and its exit from Autoutoute 81). Leave Laval by the N157 towards Le Mans, but, after 3km, turn left on the D32 to Montsûrs where turn left on to the D24 towards Mayenne, but immediately after passing over the railway line, turn right on to the D129 to Saint-Ouen. In the centre of the village, turn down the drive to the château. **Airport:** *Laval (16km)* **Station:** *Montsûrs (4km)*

The first château at La Roche-Pichemer was built in the thirteenth century as a defensive outpost, commanding the wooded valley of Deux-Evailles. The present château was constructed during the sixteenth and seventeenth centuries for the du Plessis family. One of them, René du Plessis, Marquis de Jazé, was exiled by Mazarin from the court of Louis XIII. He had the château redecorated and is responsible for the existing panelling, painted ceilings and the marble and granite fireplaces.

Perhaps he didn't like the results, because in 1645 he sold the property to the Montesson family. A century later, it was sold again. The new owner was Jean de la Haye de Bellegarde. His grand-daughter married William d'Ozouville in 1825 and it is from them that the present owner is descended.

Surrounded by woods, the granite château consists of a main courtyard and three wings in which the many high dormer windows are topped with granite finials. There is a well-kept formal garden with topiary bushes. Although the château is privately-owned, it is a listed historic monument that can be visited on request by the public. If occupied, the guest-room is not included in the tour.

FARGES-ALLICHAMPS - Saint-Amand-Montrond CENTRE - Cher

46 CHATEAU DE LA COMMANDERIE PG

♛♛♛ ★★	Twin with shower 1 C	Groups: max. 10
Farges-Allichamps, 18200 Saint-Amand-Montrond, Cher.	Double with bath 8 C-E (inc. breakfast)	Credit cards: American Express
Tel: 48 61 04 19	Total rooms: 9	English spoken
Propr: Comte & Comtesse de Jouffroy-Gonsans	Table d'hôte B (inc. aperitif & wine)	
Open: All year	Dinner only: 20.00	Tennis court
	Specialities: *Poulet à l'estrogon; Canard aux pêches.*	Golf course 40km
		Château Accueil
No lift		Indepen. Leading Association

36km south of Bourges. From there, take the N144. Afer 32km, at Bruère-Allichamps (the geographical centre of France), turn right into the village and cross the River Cher. The long drive to the château is 1km further, on the left. **Airport:** *Bourges (37km)* **Station:** *Saint-Amand-Montrond (12km)*

Overlooking the valley of the Cher, Château de la Commanderie is a small castle, surrounded by beautiful trees and meadows in which horses run free. Originally built in the fifteenth century, the château was acquired by the family of the Comtes de Jouffroy-Gonsans in the seventeenth century. During the French Revolution, much of the old château was destroyed, but after the Restoration it was rebuilt, incorporating what remained of the original. The result is magnificent. The elegant white building has many large windows and a single circular turret, topped with a witch's-cap roof.

The interior is just as pleasing. Almost every room is panelled. It might have been oppressive, but the Comte and Comtesse have selected furnishings that add colour and great appeal to the exceptionally light rooms. Family heirlooms are everywhere - delicate porcelain, old paintings, a harp and crystal chandeliers. The comfort and elegance of the bedrooms is complemented by the modern plumbing in their bathrooms.

We fully believed the Comtesse when she said, 'We consider our guests to be friends and provide every facility and help we can to make their stay enjoyable.'

47 CHATEAU ESTIVEAUX PG

18170 Le Châtelet-en-Berry, Cher.
Tel: 48 56 22 64
Propr: Mme Bernard de Faverges
Open: All year

Double with bath 2 B
Single 1 A
(inc. breakfast)
Total rooms: 3
(1 double & the single share a w.c.)

Table d'hôte (res. only) A
Dinner only: 20.00
Demi-pension (5 days +) B

No lift. 1 Room on the ground floor.

No credit cards
English spoken

Fishing
Tennis 1.5km
Sailing 19km

Gîtes de France

46km north-west of Montlucon. From there, take the D943. After 33km, at Culan, turn right on to the D65 to Le Châtelet. **Station:** *Saint-Amand-Montrond (23km)*

Built in 1840, this solid but pleasant-looking château is set in wooded grounds of 10 acres, with lawns and many flower beds. The arches above the doors and the corners of the house are decorated with alternating white and red stone, which with the white wooden shutters and the window-boxes adds splashes of colour to the stucco finish. The three rooms available have a shared bathroom and w.c. In the surrounding area, there are several large lakes where it is possible to bathe and sail. There are also many pleasant walks.

MARSEILLES-LES-AUBIGNY - Jouet-sur-l'Aubois CENTRE - Cher

48 CHATEAU D'AUBIGNY PG

★	Double with bath	3 B	Groups: max. 8
Marseilles-les-Aubigny, 18320 Jouet-sur-l'Aubois, Cher.	Suite (max. 4)	1 B	No credit cards
	Total rooms:	4	English & Spanish spoken
Tel: 48 76 07 59	No lift		By river
Propr: M. Laurence Corté-Charlois			Tennis 19km
	No restaurant		
Open: All year			Gîtes de France

21km north-east of Nevers. From there, take the D40. After crossing the Loire, turn right on the D220 to Jouet-sur-l'Aubois. There turn right on the D26 to Marseilles-les-Aubigny. The château is in the village.
Airport: *(18km)* **Station:** *Nevers (21km)*

This château is in a beautiful location. There are uninterrupted views across the Loire, which is 200m away at the bottom of the garden. The grounds of 8 acres contain many trees and a small field in which there is a donkey and some sheep. On one side is the River Abois and behind is the Forest of Aubigny.

In medieval times, a château that belonged to the Ducs de Nevers was built on the site. Later, there was also an abbey. Nothing of these now remain. Impressed by the beauty of the place, Comte Cervois chose to build the present château there in 1836. It is a high, three-storey building with rendered walls and, in the front, a vast number of shuttered windows through which can be seen splendid views of the river. This is not the most elegant of châteaux, but the welcome of the host is warm and the setting is superb.

Although breakfast is provided at the château, there is no restaurant. But close by in the village of Marseilles-les-Aubigny is the Auberge du Poids de Fer, where traditional fare can be enjoyed at reasonable prices.

49 CHATEAU DE LA VERRERIE PG

♛♛♛ ★★
Oizon, 18700 Aubigny-sur-Nère, Cher.
Tel: 48 58 06 91
Propr: Comte & Comtesse Antoine de Vogué
Open: 1 Apr - 31 Oct

Twin with bath	5 D
Double with bath	3 D
Total rooms:	8

Min. of 2-nights at weekends

No lift

Table d'hôte (res.only) B
Restaurant (in grounds):
Open 15 Jun - 30 Sep.
Closed on Tue.
Prix fixe: 2 menus at A
A la carte available
Specialities: *Fricassée de ris de veay à las creme; Assiette de jambon; Escalope de saumon; Noisettes de lotte; Coeur de filet de boeuf au roquefort.*

Seminars: max. 25
Groups: max. 16
Credit cards:
American Express,
Diners Club
English & German spoken

Tennis court
Horse riding
Sailing

Châteaux Hôtels Indép.
Château Accueil
Inter. Leading Association

35km south of Gièn. From there, take the D940 to Aubigny-sur-Nère. In the town, just after a major junction, turn left on to the D89. It's easy to miss, but it leads, after 10km, directly to the château. **Airport:** *Bourges (43km)* **Station:** *Gièn (35km)*

This magnificent château was built at the end of the fifteenth century by Béraud Stuart of Darnley. Set deep in a forest, it stands at the edge of a vast lake in which its Renaissance pinnacles are reflected. Inside the large central courtyard, the château appears even more beautiful. Its elegant loggia was erected in 1525 by Robert Stuart of Lennox after his return from the Italian wars. There is also a Gothic chapel and a turreted gateway.

From 1672 to 1734, the château was the home of the Duchess of Portsmouth, the beautiful mistress of the English king, Charles II. Her descendants, the dukes of Richmond, sold the property in 1842 to the Marquis de Vogué. His grandson is the present owner.

Throughout the château there are fine examples of furniture, tapestries, portraits and sculptures, dating back to the sixteenth century. There are ornate painted fireplaces and ceilings, polished wooden floors, and spacious bedrooms.

In the grounds, an eighteenth-century cottage has been converted into a pretty restaurant, La Maison d'Hélène, where traditional family recipes are served. (The restaurant is also used by members of the public visiting the château.) If reserved in advance, table d'hôte is also available in the château. Breakfast is served in the bedroom.

The Comte and Comtesse de Vogué speak very good English. (Apparently there have been English nannies at the château for generations.) They and their staff will help and advise guests on where to go and what to see in the area. For those not wanting to stray away from the château, there is an opportunity to use rowing boats, fishing tackle, bicycles and - for those who are experienced riders - horses.

50 CHATEAU DE LA BEUVRIERE PG

🛡🛡 ★★
Saint-Hilaire-de-Court,
18100 Vierzon, Cher.
Tel: 48 75 14 63, 48 75 08 14
Propr: Comte Arnaud & Comtesse Chantal de Brach
Open: 15 Mar - 10 Jan

Twin with shower	3 B
Twin with bath	6 A-B
Double with shower	1 B
Double with bath	5 A-B
Twin rooms (max. 3)	2 B
Total rooms:	17
Apartment (max. 5)	1 B

No lift

Restaurant: closed Sun evening & Monday
Chef: Dominique Fabas
Lunch: 1230-1400
Dinner: 1930-2130
Prix fixe 3 menus at A
Specialities: *Saumon fumé au château; Foie gras.*

Seminars: max. 40
Groups: max. 40
Receptions: max. 80

Credit cards:
American Express
Visa
English spoken

Tennis court
Fishing
Horse riding 7km
Golf course 25km

Châteaux Hôtels Indép.
Château Accueil
Inter. Leading Association

7km south-west of Vierzon. From there, take the N20 and, after crossing the Cher, turn right on to the D90. The entrance to the château is a short way along on the right. **Station:** *Vierzon (7km)*

Overlooking the valley of the Cher, this château was built originally in the eleventh century. It was partially destroyed during the Wars of Religion and rebuilt during the Renaissance. In 1827, the property was purchased by the Marquis de Monspey, ancestor of the present owners, Arnaud and Chantal de Brach. A charming and gracious couple, they have over the last few years totally restored and redecorated the château.

Their mammoth task has been a great success. Numerous improvements have been made, including a stepped forecourt that provides ample parking-space and a more imposing setting for this substantial château, with its sturdy towers and delightful loggia. Although much of the furniture is new, most has been carefully selected to blend well with the antique heirlooms. (The gilt folding-chairs in the breakfast room are an exception.) There are beautiful family portraits and other paintings on the walls.

Some of the ground-floor rooms have beamed ceilings; others throughout the château, including bedrooms, have intricately tiled floors. The pleasant dining room has wooden floors and a large stone fire-place.

As an historical monument, the château is open to the public and various events take place there, including art-exhibitions.

This is a château with touches of elegance which is comfortable and peaceful. At the current prices, it is also extremely good value.

51 CHATEAU DE THAUMIERS PG

♖♖♖ ★★	Twin with bath	3 C	No credit cards
Thaumiers, 18210	Double with bath	4 C	English & Spanish spoken
Charenton-du-Cher, Cher.	Suites (max. 4)	4 D	Tennis court
Tel: 48 61 81 62	Total rooms:	11	Fishing
Propr: Vicomte &			Mini-golf
Vicomtesse de Bonneval	No restaurant		Swimming pool 10km
Open: All year			Les Etapes Francois Coeur
No lift. 1 ground-floor	Seminars: max. 20		Châteaux Hôtels Indép.
room.	Groups: max. 12		Château Accueil

36km south of Bourges. From there, take the N76. After 16km, branch right on to the D953 to Thaumiers. The château is close to the centre of the village. **Airport:** *Bourges (37km)* **Station:** *Saint-Amand-Montrond (18km)*

In the first half of the fifteenth century, when the English army occupied much of France, this area was the royalist centre, bristling with châteaux to protect the heir to the throne. At that time, in the middle of the Bois de Meillant, Jean de La Forest erected a fortified tower that was to become the Château de Thaumiers. When his son completed the construction, it consisted of high buildings around a central courtyard with towers at each corner. In the eighteenth century, Henriette de Doulle, the ancestor of the present owners, remodelled the sombre fortress. To make the rooms as light as possible, two of the sides were demolished and large windows were installed. Three of the original towers remained and to these were added four smaller ones, making the château as it is today - a pretty building with seven towers. Fortunately, during the nineteenth century, the château escaped the horrors of the neo-Gothic renovators. But a great improvement was made. The park was remodelled by the landscape designer, M. de Choulet, who introduced a lake and stretches of lawn among the trees to provide the château with a suitably elegant setting.

In more recent times, the château suffered from years of neglect, but the present owners have patiently restored the roofs and the interior. Now the château is approaching its earlier magnificence. The bedrooms are comfortable and the public rooms are admirably furnished.

52 CHATEAU DE ROUSSAINVILLE H

★
28120 Illiers-Combray,
Eure-et-Loir.
Tel: 37 24 00 20
Propr: Mme Frida Pitchal Hochman
Open: All year

Double with shower	1
Double with bath	7
Single with bath	5
Total rooms:	13
Full pension (per person)	C

English & Spanish spoken

Not available for individual bookings. Open only to groups (from 10 to 20) for seminars & conferences on a full pension basis.

26km south-west of Chartres. From there, take the D921 to Illiers Combray. In the centre of the town, turn left, after the church, on to the D941 towards Bonneval, but after 600m, on the outskirts of Illiers, turn left on to the minor road that leads to Roussainville.

Built in 1890, the château replaced a much earlier building. It is set in a beautiful park that was established in the eighteenth century. Facilities include billiards, table-tennis and badminton. The restaurant provides traditional, family cooking.

53 CHATEAU DE MAILLEBOIS PG

★

Maillebois, 28170 Châteauneuf-en-Thymerais, Eure-et-Loir.
Tel: 37 48 17 01, 37 48 19 18
Propr: M. Lionel Armand-Delille
Open: All year

Total rooms: 3 D (inc. breakfast)
Reduced rates for long stays.
Apartment: 1 (max. 4)

No lift

No restaurant

No credit cards
English & German spoken

Tennis court
Fishing 1km

33km north-west of Chartres on the D939. The château is to the right in the village. **Airport:** *Chartres (33km)* **Station:** *Dreux (23km)*

Originally constructed in the fifteenth century, the château was twice modernised - at the end of the sixteenth and during the eighteenth century. Built of red and white bricks, it has unusual patterning on the exterior walls and, oddly, a clock set into the top of one of the pointed towers. The château is much used for large receptions and seminars. Two rivers flow through the vast grounds of over six hundred acres.

54 CHATEAU DE L'AULNAYE PG

⛨ ★
Route d'Alencon, 28400 Nogent-le-Rotrou, Eure-et-Loir.
Tel: 37 52 02 11
Propr: M. & Mme Dumas Milne Edwards
Open: All year

Double with shower 1 A
Double with bath 1 A
(inc. breakfast)
Total room: 2
Apartments: 3 (max. 6)

No lift
Table d'hôte on request A

No credit cards
English spoken

Fishing
Tennis court 500m
Riding 7km

Gîtes de France

Route d'Alencon is the D955, travelling north-west from Nogent-le-Rotrou towards Alencon. Shortly after the road forks left from the N23, turn right, following the signs to the château. **Airport:** *Chartres (47km)* **Station:** *Nogent-le-Rotrou (1.5km)*

Originally built in the eighteenth century as a hunting lodge, the building was converted a hundred years later into a palatial family-home, with a billiard-room and, on the first floor, six bedrooms, each with a private bathroom. Further alterations were made at the end of the nineteenth century by the then owner, Alphonse Milne Edwards, the Curator of the Natural History Museum in Paris. To his summer residence he added four more bedrooms and bathrooms on the second floor, under the roof.

The present owners have created a holiday apartment and a self-contained bedroom on both the first and the second floors. In the pretty grounds of over 15 acres there are lawns, rhododendrons and azaleas. The private lake teems with carp, tench and roach.

AZAY-LE-RIDEAU CENTRE - Indre-et-Loire

58 CHATEAU DU GERFAUT PG

♛♛♛ ★
37190 Azay-le-Rideau,
Indre- et-Loire.
Tel: 47 45 40 16
Propr: Marquis & Marquise de Chénerilles
Open: All year

Twin with shower	1 B	
Double with bath	3 B-C	
Double with shower	2 B	
(inc. breakfast)		
Total rooms:	6	

No lift

Table d'hôte on reservation

No credit cards
English & German spoken

Tennis court
Golf course 12km

Châteaux Accueil

24km south-west of Tours. From there, take the D751 towards Azay-le-Rideau. 2km before the town and immediately before a Total petrol station, turn right down a long private road that passes through fields and leads to the château. It is easy to miss and is not well sign-posted. **Airport:** *Tours (24km)* **Station:** *Tours*

In about 1810, Jerome Bonaparte, the brother of Napoleon, gave the vast Villandry estate as settlement of a debt to a banker called Hainguerlot. With the exception of the château, which was sold in 1880, the estate has remained in his family's possession. In 1910, Comte Jean de Sabian-Ponteves - grandfather of the present owner - built a hunting-lodge close to the forest, which had been a royal hunting-ground. He called the château 'Gerfaut', the French name for the gyrfalcons used by the hunters.

It is an impressive, stone building, with a double flight of steps sweeping up to the front door. The Marquis de Chénerilles is a charming, friendly host, who makes his guests extremely welcome.

The massive entrance hall has much wooden panelling and wide oak stairs. On one side is an enormous display of stags' heads mounted on the wall; on the other side there is an equally large collection of wild boars' heads. Off the hall is a huge sitting-room with windows overlooking the garden, both at the front and at the back. Although the room is full of delightful furniture and fascinating objects, it is difficult not to be most impressed by the idiocies of early twentieth-century plumbing. An enormous ancient central-heating boiler stands in front of the elaborate fire-place; a radiator blocks one of a pair of doors.

The bedrooms are on the first and second floors. They are pleasant and well decorated in a simple style. Much of their furnishings are antique. On both landings there is something that looks like a bidet - they were apparently installed when the house was built to provide the servants cleaning the corridors with a supply of water.

This château has an informal, friendly atmosphere that makes it a delightful place to stay.

59 CHATEAU D'ARTANNES -

Le Palais des Archèveques de Tours PG

♔♔ ★★
Artannes-sur-Indre, 37260 Monts, Indre-et-Loire.
Tel: 47 65 70 60
Telex: 752 435 F
Propr: M. & Mme Bernard Hoffmann
Director: Mme J. Elisabeth Hartsema
Open: All year

Total rooms: 7 F

No lift

Table d'hôte on request B

Seminars: max. 25
Groups: max. 24
Credit cards: Visa
English, German & Italian spoken

Fishing 500m
Horse riding 500m
Tennis courts 3km
Swimming pool 10km

14km south-east of Tours. From there, take the D751. After 11.5km, turn left on to the D8. Turn left into Artannes. In the centre of the village, after a sharp right turn, the château is on the left. **Airport:** *Tours (17km)* **Station:** *Tours (14km)*

Until the door was sealed, it was possible to walk from a room in the château directly into the parish church. This was because, from the fifteenth century, the house was the summer palace of the Archbishop of Tours. That came to an end during the French Revolution when the property was seized and sold.

The present owners have decided to open their home for business seminars and vacations. It is an imposing château with small but pleasant grounds. As far as possible, original wall hangings and fixtures have been retained. As a result, the sitting-room and dining room are rather dark but not unpleasant. The bedrooms have been decorated using cheerful colour schemes, although one room with a superb antique four-poster bed has been left much as it was. The elegance of the bathrooms is somewhat marred by the new two-tone baths, toilets and tiles. All the rooms are enormous and many have their own sitting-room. At the top of the house is an old grain-store that is also being converted into suites. Though short on windows, they will offer unusual, if expensive, accommodation.

ARTANNES-SUR-INDRE - Monts | CENTRE - Indre-et-Loire

60 CHATEAU LA MOTHE PG

♛♛★	Double with bath 2 B	Seminars: max. 30
Artannes-sur-Indre, 37260 Monts, Indre-et-Loire.	Twin rooms with bath 1 B	No credit cards
Tel: 47 26 80 18	Total rooms: 3	English spoken
Propr: M. Christian & Mme Béatrice Lamy	Table d'hôte on request (min. 4 hrs notice) A	River bathing
Open: All year		Fishing
		Riding Centre 1Km
		Tennis court 3km
No lift		Gîtes de France

14km south-east of Tours. From there, take the D751. After 11.5km, turn left on to the D8. Turn left into Artannes. In the centre of the village, when the main road takes a sharp right turn, keep straight on. Take the first right down a narrow lane and then first left. The narrow entrance to the château is on right. **Airport:** *Tours (17km)* **Station:** *Tours (14km)*

Burnt down during the French Revolution, this château was rebuilt shortly afterwards incorporating what remained of the original - including a circular tower dating from the fifteenth century. At the beginning of this century, André Maginot (creator of the 'Maginot Line') gave the château to his mistress who threw many spectacular parties there.

Those days have gone. The château is now the family home of M. and Mme Lamy and their three children. They purchased La Mothe at the beginning of 1989.

This grey vine-clad building is set amidst plane trees in an idyllic spot by the banks of the Indre. A heavy old oak-door in the tower leads to circular steps which wind their way up to the bedrooms. They are delightful - simply decorated and furnished with antiques. The bathrooms are excellent and very large, although the plumbing is somewhat eccentric - when our bath slowly emptied, it first filled the bidet! An enormous table runs almost the entire length of the attractive dining room, which is full of fascinating objets d'art and family memorabilia. Outside is a terrace overlooking the moat and the meandering river. Facilities, including a small boat and fish pond, are provided for anglers. There are also many extremely pleasant walks in this beautiful and relatively unknown location.

Top: **Château de la Commanderie** (46) Cher (Centre)
Bottom: **Château de Marcay** (70) Indre-et-Loire (Centre)

Top: **Domaine de Beauvois** (69) Indre-et-Loire (Centre)
Bottom: **Château d'Artigny** (71) Indre-et-Loire (Centre)

BEAUMONT-EN-VERON - Chinon CENTRE - Indre-et-Loire

61 CHATEAU DE COULAINE PG

♥♥♥
Beaumont-en-Veron, 37420
Avoine, Indre-et-Loire.
Tel: 47 93 01 27
Propr: Marquis & Marquise de Bonnaventure
Open: Easter - 31 Oct

No lift

Twin with bath	2 B
Double with shower & distant w.c.	1 A
Double with bath	1 B
(inc. breakfast)	
Total rooms:	4
Apartment (max. 4)	1

Table d'hôte (res. only) A
Dinner at 2000

No credit cards

River 500m
Swimming pool 2km
Tennis court 2km
Horse riding 2km

Gîtes de France

4km west of Chinon. From there, take the D749, crossing over the D151. The château is on the right, just before a sharp bend in the road. **Airport:** *Tours (45km)* **Station:** *Port-Bouler (4km)*

Only a field separates this medieval château from the busy main road to Chinon. Approaching it is like entering into a time-warp, which is hardly surprising because it has changed little since it was built in 1470 - twenty-two years before Columbus set off on his first voyage across the Atlantic.

The drive passes through an avenue of trees and then past a farm-yard and small, derelict chapel. The towering château has crumbling sandstone carvings around the windows and doors. Above the doorway are the eroded arms of the Craon family - early owners of the château. It is the kind of place where, you imagine, rooks will flap off cawing into the gloom, as weary travellers climb up the time-worn steps and bang on the heavy, dilapidated front door.

Inside, an apparently endless flight of ancient white-stone steps winds up through the tower. On the first floor is the gloomy dining room, which is full of dark heavy furniture, stuffed animal heads and oil paintings, blackened with age.

The bedrooms are on the next floor. The circular staircase leads to a high corridor, in which the ceiling's beams are painted with heraldic motifs. At intervals, grimacing gargoyles leer down. The walls are dark green and brown; the floor is laid with stone tiles. Some effort has been made to modernise the bedrooms, but obviously on a limited budget. However, they are all comfortable and clean, with plenty of hot water. The cheapest room has a toilet at the end of the long corridor. The ancient lavatory has an unusual flushing system. When the adjacent lever is pulled, a trap opens deep inside the pan, there is a sound that can be heard throughout the château, and everything drops down a deep black hole.

The Marquise de Bonnaventure is shy but helpful. She speaks very little English, but copes patiently with phrase-book French.

Travellers wanting luxury should avoid this place; those seeking an authentic, unusual and memorable experience will love it.

62 CHATEAU DE DANZAY PG

♛♛ ★★
Beaumont-en-Veron, 37420
Avoine, Indre-et-Loire.
Tel: 47 58 46 86
Propr: M. Jacques & Mme Josiane Sarfati
Open: 1 Apr - 31 Oct

No lift

Twin with bath	1 D
Double with bath	5 C-E
Suite (max. 3)	1 E
Total rooms:	7

No restaurant

Credit cards:
Visa
English & Italian spoken

Fishing 1km
Swimming pool 2km
Tennis court 2km
Horse riding 2km
Golf course 12km

Châteaux Hôtels Indép.
Château Accueil
Gîtes de France

5km west of Chinon. From there, take the D749 towards Bourgueil. After 4km, the road bends sharply to the right. At this point go straight on. After 900 m, turn right along a road that leads to the château. **Airport:** *Tours (46km)* **Station:** *Port-Bouler (5km)*

Surrounded by vineyards and open fields, Château de Danzay is compact and unassuming. It has been restored with great sensitivity by Jacques and Josiane Sarfati, who have managed to preserve the essence of the fifteenth-century building while endowing it with modern comforts. The white stone walls have been left uncovered, the huge beams have been cleaned, and, on the ground floor, the bare stone floors are polished. At both ends of the long hall, there are large open fire-places. There is no clutter; the fabrics are plain; the furniture is simple, antique and kept to a minimum. The resulting simplicity is delightful.

All the bedrooms have fitted carpets and comfortable beds, one of which is a four-poster. The bathrooms are luxurious. The chapel has been converted into a very modern apartment. Its bedroom has white carpet and coverings, white walls, a floor-to-ceiling mirror and an ultra-modern bathroom area.

The Sarfatis are an interesting and talented couple who make guests feel very welcome in their unique home. Very pleasant!

CINQ-MARS-LA-PILE CENTRE - Indre-et-Loire

63 CHATEAU DE CINQ-MARS PG

Cinq-Mars-la-Pile, 37130 Langeais, Indre-et-Loire.
Tel: 47 96 40 49
Propr: Mme Nicolas Untersteller
Open: 1 Mar - 31 Dec

Double with bath	3 C
Suite (max. 5)	1 D
Total rooms:	4

No lift. 3 ground-floor rooms.

No restaurant

No credit cards

Tennis court 1km
Fishing 1km
Golf course 18km

Château Accueil
Les Etapes Francois Coeur

17km west of Tours. From there, take the N152 along the north bank of the Loire. In Cinq-Mars turn right to the château. **Airport:** *Tours (17km)* **Station:** *Langeais (4km) & Tours*

The Marquis de Cinq-Mars was beheaded in 1642 at the age of twenty-two for having conspired with the Spaniards to overthrow Richelieu. The Cardinal then ordered the seizure and destruction of the Marquis's eleventh-century castle. Only two towers and the dry moat remain.

Much later, a long low house was built in the grounds. This is the home of the ceramic artist, Mme Nicolas Untersteller. Now an elderly lady, she clearly enjoys meeting new people and is most hospitable. Her home-made walnut brandy is to be treated with caution!

In the main room, where breakfast is served, the floor is polished slate. There is a giant stone fireplace and a huge arched window looking out into the surrounding woods. The bedrooms are comfortable with twin beds, covered with bright cotton bedspreads. There are pretty rugs on the slate-floor and cheerful flower paintings on the walls. Outside, there is a secluded garden where peacocks roam the soft green lawns under the giant cypress trees. The Château is not luxurious but it is charming and the setting is superb.

JOUE-LES-TOURS CENTRE - Indre-et-Loire

64 CHATEAU DE BEAULIEU H

⛉ ★★★
Route de l'Epend, 27200 Joué-lès-Tours, Indre-et-Loire.
Tel: 47 53 20 26
Propr: M. & Mme Jean-Pierre Lozay
Open: All year

Twin with bath	7 B-C
Double with shower	4 B-C
Double with bath	8 B-C
Total rooms:	19
(10 rooms in annexe)	

No lift. 3 gd. fl. rooms

Restaurant: Open daily
Chef: M. Jean-Pierre Lozay, maître cuisinier de France
Lunch: 1215 - 1400
Dinner: 1915 - 2115
Prix fixe: Menus at A & B
A la carte available
Demi-pension (3 days+) D
Specialities: *Cassolette de petits gris frais au beurre d'escargots; Pigeon farci aux cèpes; Choux farcis aux langoustines et son coulis; Saumon fumé maison.*

Seminars: max. 30
Groups: max. 40
Receptions: max. 80
Credit cards: Visa
English spoken

Swimming pool
Tennis club
Golf course 4km
Horse riding 4km

Châteaux Hôtels Indép.
Relais du Silence
Les Cuisiniers et Hôteliers de Métier, Hostellerie du Vignoble Francais

5km south-west of Tours. Take the Rue Giraudeau and cross the Cher. Keep stright on, along the D86. Soon after the end of the dual carriageway, take the first right - the D207. It is a very narrow road, much used as a short-cut, so be careful. The château, hidden behind a high wall, is on the right. **Airport:** *Tours (8km)* **Station:** *Tours (5km)*

This elegant eighteenth-century mansion stands on a hillside overlooking formal gardens and the Cher valley. The entrance is at the side, up a steep flight of stone stairs. Once inside, it is obvious that this is a busy and efficient hotel. To the left of the main corridor is the reception area, which also serves in the evening as the bar and lounge. It is furnished with comfortable, squashy, modern chairs.

To the right of the corridor are the two dining rooms, both of which overlook the garden. With crisp white napery and large bowls of fresh flowers on every table, this is the stage where each evening Jean-Pierre Lozay's spectacular creations are presented. Not surprisingly, the restaurant appears always to be full.

In the corridor is a somewhat incongruous collection of halberds, opposite the flight of stairs that leads to the bedrooms. These are comfortable and immaculate.

All the staff are helpful. Mme Lozay is a charming and efficient Scot.

65 CHATEAU DE LA CELLE-GUENAND PG

La Celle-Guenand, 37350 Le Grand-Pressigny, Indre-et-Loire.	Total rooms: 6 B (inc. breakfast)	No restaurant
Tel: 47 94 94 49	Some share bathroom and w.c.	No credit cards
Propr: Mme Jane de l'Aigle	No lift	Tennis court 6km Swimming pool 10km
Open: All year		Gîtes de France

42km north-east of Châtellerault. From there, take the D725 eastwards through la Roche-Posay to just beyond Preuilly-sur-Claise (36km). Then turn left on to the D50 to La Celle-Guenand. The château is in the centre of the village. **Airport:** *Tours (53km)* **Station:** *Châtellerault (42km)*

This castle was constructed in the fourteenth century on the foundations of an even earlier fortress. Much of the interior was destroyed during the Revolution. A few attempts have been made in the past to restore it, but when the present owners took over, they were faced with a mammoth task. Now their hard work is bearing fruit and a magnificent ancient building is being reimbued with life. Although in the middle of the village, it is set in its own wooded parkland of over six acres.

As work was still in progress, we cannot give a detailed description. We welcome reports.

66 CHATEAU DE CHEMILLY PG

⛨ ★
RN 152, 37130 Langeais, Indre-et-Loire.
Tel: 47 96 55 06
Propr: Mme LeBlanc
Open: All year

Twin with shower	1 B
Double with bath	2 B
Total rooms:	3

No lift

No restaurant

Seminars: max. 20
No credit cards

Fishing
Swimming pool 3km
Tennis court 3km

Gîtes de France

25km west of Tours. From there, take the N152 along the north bank of the Loire to Langeais. Turn right into the village and take the road to the right (the D16). Twice roads turn off to the left, but keep to the right. The château is 2.5km further on the right. **Airport:** *Tours (28km)* **Station:** *Langeais or Tours (25km)*

Driving along through the woods, one catches glimpses of Château de Chemilly, sitting primly above a small lake with a river flowing gently by. It is a beautiful, 18th-century building that was bought in early 1987 by M. and Mme LeBlanc and is being renovated to a very high standard. The bedrooms are large and luxurious. The walls are covered with padded fabric; the paintwork is a blend of two-toning colours which produces an interesting ageing effect; and the fabric on the four-poster beds matches the curtains. The effect is most pleasing. The public rooms seemed a little less inviting, but they may well have changed since we visited.

Madame LeBlanc is a chic and charming hostess, who is anxious to ensure that guests enjoy their stay. (She has started to learn English.)

The grounds are very beautiful. To the east of the château is a charming chapel, which contains a marble altar from the time of Louis XIV. Beyond the lake is a classical orangery, which Mme Leblanc plans to convert into guest rooms.

LARCAY CENTRE - Indre-et-Loire

67 CHATEAU DE LARCAY PG

⛨ ★
37270 Larcay, Indre-et-Loire.
Tel: 47 50 39 39
Propr: M. André & Mme Colette Le Sage
Open: Easter - 31 Oct

No lift

Twin with shower	1	B
Twin with bath	2	B-C
Double with bath	2	B-C
Suite (max. 4)	1	C
Total rooms:	6	

No restaurant

Groups: max. 14 (4 days+)
No credit cards
English & Italian spoken

Tennis court 500m
Swimming pool 2km
Golf course 10km

Gîtes de France

8km east of Tours. From there, take the N76, along the south bank of the Cher. Larcay is 3km after passing under Autoroute 10. At the crossroads in the village, turn right up the hill. Almost immediately, turn right into the drive to the château. **Airport:** *Tours (12km)* **Station:** *Tours (8km)*

Built in 1830 in the Romantic style, Château de Larcay has a simple elegance that is most attractive. Four splendid towers flank each corner and in the centre of the facade, above the main entrance, is a niche containing a statue of Diana, the original of which is in the Louvre. The site is very ancient, dating back to Roman times, and many châteaux have been built there. The previous one was destroyed during the French Revolution, but a Renaissance chapel and an ancient tower still survive. Beneath the château is a vast network of underground tunnels, which were once used to store wine.

The entrance hall is dominated by an enormous oak spiral staircase, which leans crazily to one side - though it is quite safe! Many of the rooms are unexpectedly small, but extremely cosy. The guest rooms are on the second and third floors. They are all decorated in a rather uninspired but comfortable style. M. and Mme Le Sage acquired the château in 1987 and they have been busy modernising it. They are excellent hosts, who love their new home and enjoy sharing it. M. Le Sage is a wine expert and may be tempted to show guests his private wine-cellar. The main salon is decorated with beautiful wall paintings in an 18th century style.

The grounds are extensive and the views over the Cher are most pleasing. Close to Tours, this is a pleasant place to stay while exploring the region.

68 CHATEAU DES REAUX PG

🛡🛡🛡 ★★ 🍷
Le Port-Boulet, 37140 Bourgueil, Indre-et-Loire.
Tel: 47 95 14 40
Propr: M. Jean-Luc & Mme Florence Goupil de Bouillé
Open: All year

No lift

Double with bath 17 B-E
12 in the château,
5 in converted buildings

Table d'hôte on request A

Seminars: max. 25
Groups: max. 30
No credit cards

English & German spoken

Fishing 2km
Tennis courts 2km
Horse riding 5km
Golf course 12km

Châteaux Hôtels Indép.
Château Accueil

44km west of Tours. From there, take the N152 along the north bank of the Loire. After the junction with the D749, after 43km, take the first right, which leads to the château. **Airport:** *Tours (45km)* **Station:** *Saumur (19km)*

Exquisitely pretty, Château des Réaux is a romantic gem. Its origins go back to 1435, when Jean Briconnet, the first mayor of Tours, bought the remains of an ancient fortress, called Le Plessis-Rideau. His son Guillaume, who was the grand-father of the Duc de Sully, turned the ruins into a spectacular castle. The weather has faded the terracotta and white bricks that chequer the cluster of round and square towers - so adding to this moated château's charm.

In 1651, Plessis-Rideau was sold to the famous essayist and historian, Gédéon Tallemant des Réaux. He not only brought new life and distinction to the château, he gave it his name. In 1897, the grand-father of the present owners bought des Réaux, which was in a sorry state. The best part of a century has been given to restoring one of the treasures of medieval France.

The interior is just as delightful as the facade. There are heavily beamed ceilings, highly polished stone and tile floors, an ornately carved wooden fireplace, and room after room full of interesting objects, beautiful old furniture, precious tapestries and marvellous paintings. Everything has been chosen with flair and arranged with great style. Yet it has not been done for show or as an exhibition, but to create a beautiful, cultured home.

The walls of the entrance hall have been covered with a pretty pastel-blue fabric in a modern design. Similar material has been used with great effect in some of the bedrooms, all of which are charmingly and luxuriously furnished. The dining room, which is on the first floor, is superb - warm terracotta-coloured walls, a high beamed ceiling, tall windows, an elegant stone fire-place, a long bow-ended table surrounded by comfortable high-backed chairs in a delicate patterned fabric, an arrangement of fresh flowers. It is definitely a room in which to linger.

And so is the château. Jean-Luc Goupil de Bouillé is a witty and urbane host; Florence Goupil de Bouillé is energetic and creative. They form a perfect team. Everything runs efficiently in an atmosphere that is relaxed and friendly. A stay in their home is a most rewarding experience. Many better-known places are widely advertised as being an ideal base from which to explore the Loire Valley. We know of nowhere better than Château des Réaux.

69 DOMAINE DE BEAUVOIS H

⛨⛨ ★★★
Route de Cléré, B.P.27, 37230 Luynes, Indre-et-Loire.
Tel: 47 55 50 11
Telex: 750 204 F
Fax: 47 55 50 11
Propr: M. René Traversac (a Grandes Etapes Francaises)
Direc: M. Jean Claude Taupin
Open: mid-Mar - mid-Jan

Twin with bath	14 C-F
Double with bath	16 C-F
Suites (max. 5)	8 G-I
Total rooms:	38

Lift. 7 ground-floor rooms.

Restaurant: Open daily
Chef: M. Daniel Tauvel
Lunch: 1230 - 1415
Dinner: 1930 - 2115
Prix fixe: Menus at A & B
A la carte available
Demi-pension on request

Seminars: max. 60
Groups: max. 25
Credit cards:
Eurocard
Visa
English, German, Italian & Spanish spoken

Swimming pool
Tennis court
Fishing
Canoeing
Golf course 5 km

Relais & Châteaux

15km west of Tours and the A10. From Tours, take the N152 along the north bank of the Loire towards Saumur. At Port de Luynes, turn right on the D49 through Luynes and to the château, which is well sign-posted. **Airport:** *Tours (20km)* **Station:** *Tours (15km)*

During the French Revolution, the Comtesse de la Beraudière managed to save most of the Beauvois estate. In 1789 a decree was promulgated that the estates of the aristocrats who had left the country or fought against the revolution would be forfeited. Her royalist husband fled, but the Comtesse stayed at Beauvois and obtained a Certificate of Non-Emigration allowing her to retain her lands. An order was passed, however, demanding the demolition of the château's towers, which were seen as a symbol of the old feudal system.

One of these fifteenth-century towers survived - perhaps because the mob could not have pulled them all down without destroying the seventeenth-century buildings attached to them. So now the château consists of three large mansard-roofed wings stemming from a central tower with a pointed turret. Surrounded by a wooded park of over 350 acres, Domaine de Beauvois stands on a hillside, overlooking its lake, water-meadows and the forest beyond. In 1967 the château was bought by René Traversac, France's saviour of decaying historic buildings, and transformed by him into an elegant hotel.

Managed by Jean Claude Taupin with great charm and efficiency, Beauvois has the amenities and facilities to cater for even the most demanding of guests. On the ground floor, there are several attractive lounge areas with fresh flowers everywhere, adding their colour and perfume to the hotel's elegant ambiance. There is a dining room so spacious that some will find it impersonal. With white-and-black tiled floors, it is stylishly decorated with plain terracotta walls, on one of which is a huge tapestry. The windows look out over the terrace with its ornamental reflecting pool to the wooded valley beyond. The food matches the surroundings. The chef, Daniel Tauvel, has worked at Beauvois since it became a hotel and his inventive cuisine has been awarded a Michelin rosette.

The bedrooms are all different. Every effort has been made to retain the atmosphere of an old country house, although, as in all of the Grandes Etapes Francaises hotels, some heavily-patterned fabrics have been used. The bathrooms are luxuriously furnished, including, for those who can't go anywhere without them, a telephone.

At Beauvois, everything possible seems to be done to ensure the guests' comfort. In previous centuries, things were not always so. It is said that Louis XIII stayed in one of the bedrooms in the tower but, because it was so hot, he spent half the night sleeping outside on the grass.

MARCAY - Chinon CENTRE - Indre-et-Loire

70 CHATEAU DE MARCAY H

♔♔ ★★★
Marcay, 37500 Chinon,
Indre-et-Loire.
Tel: 47 93 03 47
Telex: 751 475 F
Propr: M. Philippe Mollard
Open: mid-Mar - mid-Jan

Twin with shower	6	C
Twin with bath	7	E
Double with shower	4	C
Double with bath	18	D-E
Suites	3	F
Total rooms:	38	

(27 rooms in the château. 11 in the pavilion annexe)

Lift. 13 ground-floor rooms.

Restaurant: Open daily
Chef: M. Gerard Come
Lunch: 1230 - 1430
Dinner: 1930 - 2130
Prix fixe: Menus at A & B
A la carte available
Demi-pension C-E
Specialities: *Oeufs à la coque à la purée de morilles; Crépinettes de ris de veau farcies au foie gras; Rosace de lotte et de courgettes au coulis de langoustines; Agneau de lait à l'ail doux; Tarte chaude aux pommes et son beurre au cidre.*

Seminars: max. 50
Groups: max. 70
Credit cards:
American Express
Diners Club
Visa
English, German & Spanish spoken

Swimming pool
Tennis courts
Helipad
Golf course 25km

Relais & Châteaux

7km south of Chinon. Cross over the River Vienne on the D749. At the junction, turn right on to the D751. Where this meets the D759, turn left. After 4.5km, turn left to Marcay. **Airport:** *Tours (56km)* **Station:** *Chinon (7km)*

Seen from the distance, this château conjures up images of fair damsels in need of rescue. Built of white stone, it has at either end a large round tower with a black pointed turret and authentic machicolations. It looks every inch the fairy-tale castle.

When it was originally built in 1150, the château was much larger and had an outer wall that enclosed the whole village, but being such an important military stronghold it was frequently attacked. By the beginning of the seventeenth century it had been reduced to its present size.

After much restoration, the château was opened as an hotel in 1971. It is a very efficient place, with a discreet and attentive staff. Everywhere is decorated with style and much effort has been made to retain an atmosphere of grandeur, combined with comfort. Many of the bedrooms are impressive, though some are decorated with matching bold-patterned wall-coverings, curtains and bedcovers that are overwhelming. The modern extension blends in satisfactorily and contains eleven smaller bedrooms.

The lounge is pleasant, with fresh flowers, polished wood-block floors and a high ceiling that has jade-green painted beams. The dining room was obviously designed to create a sense of occasion - the combination of startling modern wallpaper, old oak beams, an enormous tapestry and dining-chairs upholstered in terracotta-coloured fabric is loved by some and hated by others. The food, however, seems to meet with everyone's approval, including Michelin which has awarded a rosette. The wine-list is extensive, including a fine Val de Loire selection. On warm summer evenings, dinner is also served on the terrace.

71 CHATEAU D'ARTIGNY H

⛨⛨ ★★★
Route d'Azay-le-Rideau, 37250 Montbazon, Indre-et-Loire.
Tel: 47 26 24 24
Telex: 750 900 F
Propr: M. René Traversac (a Grandes Etapes Francaises)
Direc: M. Alain Rabier
Open: 11 Jan-30 Nov

Twin with shower	2	C
Twin with bath	28	C-F
Double with bath	16	C-F
Suites	7	F
Total rooms:	46	

2 lifts. 7 ground-floor rooms.

Restaurant: Open daily
Chef: M. Francis Maignaut
Lunch: 1215 - 1415
Dinner: 1915 - 2115
Prix fixe: Menus at B
A la carte available
Demi-pension C-E
Specialities: *Foie gras frais de canard mariné et poché au vin de Bonnezeaux; Composé de homard, rouget, barbet et moelle au clair de lie fine; Rôti de pigeon et foie gras au vin de Banyuls, rubans de légumes.* (The carte changes three times a year.)

Seminars: max. 80
Groups: max. 20
Credit cards: Visa
English, German & Spanish spoken

Swimming pool
Tennis courts
Practice golf
Golf course 15km

Relais & Châteaux

13km south of Tours. From there, take the N10 to Montbazon, where turn right on to the D17 towards Azay-le-Rideau. 2km further on the left is the drive to the château. **Airport:** *Tours (16km)* **Station:** *Tours (13km)*

Château d'Artigny is not what it seems. Described in some guide-books as being an eighteenth-century castle, it was actually built in the 1920s as the summer-home of Francois Coty, the perfumier. For twelve years, he employed the best master-builders and artists of the age to construct his spectacular house, modelled externally on the Château de Champlatreux in the Valley of the Oise, but fitted out inside to his personal whim. The massive kitchens are all in the basement, so that no smells of cooking would waft into the spectacular public rooms.

Coty's grandiose plans for the château and its pavilions had not been completed when he died in 1934. Five years later, war broke out and the château was occupied first by the French Naval Minister and shortly afterwards by German soldiers. After the war, Coty's children handed the château over to the Hospital of Tours so that it could be used as an annexe for the war-wounded. It was only in 1959 that the property was vacated and sold. The purchaser was René Traversac. It was twelve years before the restoration, completion and adaptation of the building into a luxury hotel was complete.

Restored to its opulent splendour, it impresses, as Coty had intended it should. The entrance hall is stunning - the white stone walls, floor, columns and vast curved flight of polished limestone stairs are bathed in light from the many windows that extend from floor to ceiling. A colossal arrangement of flowers stands on an ormolu-decorated table. The hall leads to a sumptuous Regency room, with gilded mirror and chandeliers. This is where balls and musical soirées are held. Nearby is the bar and lounge - a room ornate with gold rococo embellishments and furnished with comfortable modern arm-chairs, a grand piano and a giant red Turkish carpet. Next door is the breathtaking dining room. It is large, round and painted jade-green with intricate gilded embellishments around the panelling and coving. Mock Corinthian columns rise to the elaborate ceiling. Between them, the arched windows look out over the Valley of the Indre.

Upstairs, the salon above the dining room, is even more astonishing. Its domed ceiling is decorated with a trompe l'oeil fresco. Painted by C. Hoffbauer, it depicts Coty and friends, including the Aga Khan, standing on balconies during a costume ball.

After all this spectacle and space, many of the bedrooms in both the château and the nearby pavilion seem surprisingly small. But for those who need more spacious accommodation, there are the luxurious suites.

Because of the many seminars held there, Château d'Artigny is much used by businessmen. This might have meant that the atmosphere was cold and impersonal. It isn't - thanks to the charm and helpfulness of the attentive staff. The food too is good, and worthy of the Michelin rosette.

72 DOMAINE DE LA TORTINIERE H

♥♥ ★★★
Les Gués de Veigné, 37250 Montbazon, Indre-et-Loire.
Tel: 47 26 00 19
Telex: 752 186 F
Propr: Famille Capron
Direc: Mme Denise Olivereau- Capron
Open: 1 Mar - 20 Dec

Twin with bath	6	B-D
Twin with shower	1	B
Double with bath	7	B-C
Suites (max 4)	7	D-E
Total rooms:	21	

No lift. 5 ground-floor rooms in an annexe.

Restaurant: In Mar & after 15 Oct, closed on Tue and Wed morning
Chef: M. C. Laize
Lunch: 1200 - 1330
Dinner: 1915 - 2100
Prix fixe 1 menu at B
Demi-pension (3 days+) C-E
Specialities: *Saumon frais gros sel, ses légumes nouveaux; Blanc de turbot à la mode de boeuf; Pigeonneau de touraine rôti au miel; Escalope de foie gras aux petities cérales; Gratin de framboises aux amandes.*

Seminars: max. 30
Groups: max. 20
Credit cards: Visa
English, German, Italian & Spanish spoken

Cookery course
Swimming pool
Tennis court
Golf course 16km

Châteaux Hôtels Indép.
Relais du Silence

11km south of Tours. From there, take the D10. At Les Gués de Veigné, turn right on the D27. The château is well sign-posted. **Airport:** *Tours (14km)* **Station:** *Tours (11km)*

An enormous variety of trees grow in the hundred acres of delightful parkland surrounding the Domaine de la Tortinière. The many rare species include two three-headed sophoras, a sequoia, and two cedars of Lebanon, planted in 1795. That was long before the present château was built. It was not until 1861 that the white-stoned, turreted house was designed and constructed by Pauline Dalloz, the widow of the famous lawyer who compiled France's Code of Civil Law. Because she was inspired by the beautiful Renaissance buildings in the area, the design included none of the neo-Gothic horrors so popular at the time.

Over the years, the château changed ownership three times remaining always a large, family home. Its brief hour of glory was in 1870 when the document announcing the surrender of Tours to the invading German army was signed in its sitting-room. In 1954, M. and Mme Capron bought La Tortinière and, the following year, turned it into a hotel. It is run now by one of their daughters, Denise Olivereau-Capron, helped by her three children - Sophie, Xavier and Gregoire.

The bedrooms are all different and comfortable. Some are in the château and others in the converted stable block. The suites are in the three pavilions close by.

For many years the cuisine has been a strong feature of La Tortinière, although it is unfortunate that only one, somewhat expensive, menu is available. The wine list, however, is reasonable and includes many wines from the Loire region. The dining room is in what was once an orangery. Fresh flowers are on every table and the service is good, but the metal framed furniture is unnecessarily austere, creating an atmosphere more of a patio than of an expensive restaurant.

A five-day 'Château Country Cooking Course' is held at La Tortinière in March/April and October/November. In addition to classes on the regional cuisine, there are visits to several local châteaux to dine with their owners. The course, which includes the cost of all meals and wine, is expensive.

MONTPOUPON - Montrésor CENTRE - Indre-et-Loire

73 CHATEAU DE MONTPOUPON PG

⛨⛨ ★	Twin with bath	2 C	Table d'hôte on request A (inc. wine and aperitif)
Ceré-la-Ronde, 37460 Montrésor, Indre-et-Loire.	Single with bath	3 B	
Tel: 47 94 23 62, 47 94 30 77	Double with bath	1 C	
Propr: Mlle de la Motte Saint-Pierre	Suites	2 D	Groups: max. 10
Open: 1 Mar - 31 Oct	Total rooms:	8	No credit cards
	No lift		English & Spanish spoken

41km south of Blois. From there, take the D764. The château is on the right-hand side of the road. **Airport:** *Blois (47km)* **Station:** *Loches (20km)*

This ancient walled fortress is planted on a hill overlooking what was the main trade-route to Spain. It still contains a thirteenth-century tower, a fifteenth-century house, an ancient kitchen and a museum of hunting. There are watchtowers, mullion windows, a gate-house, towers, a chapel and a crenellated outer wall - everything any child could wish to find in the most perfect toy castle.

The bedrooms are comfortable and well furnished. One is a Louis XVI room and another has a bed canopied with green damask. The bathrooms are somewhat ancient, but clean and serviceable. There are ornate stone fire-places and in the dining room a remarkable tapestry. On the first floor, there is a library with displays of children's clothes, dolls and games.

This fascinating château has belonged to the Motte Saint-Pierre family since 1857. It is well worth a visit.

NAZELLES - Amboise CENTRE - Indre-et-Loire

74 CHATEAU LA HUBERDIERE PG

★
Nazelles, 37400 Amboise, Indre-et-Loire.
Tel: 47 57 39 32
Propr: Mme Beatrice Sandrier
Open: All year

No lift

Twin with bath	3	B-C
Double with bath	2	B-C
Suite	1	C
Total rooms:	6	
Apartments (max. 5)	1	

Table d'hôte on request A

Groups: max. 14
No credit cards
English, German & Italian spoken

Stabling
Fishing
Tennis court 3km
Swimming pool 7km

Château Accueil
Gîtes de France
Les Etapes Francois Coeur

6km north of Amboise. From the centre of the town, cross the Loire to the northern bank by the D5 to Nazelles. Turn left on to the D1. After 1km, just before the village of Bardouillière, turn right on to the D79 and immediately right again through the village of Vaugadeland. The château is on the left. **Airport:** *Tours (32km)* **Station:** *Amboise (6km)*

The narrow road that winds up to this seventeenth-century hunting-lodge passes through delightful countryside. La Huberdière is on the slopes of a hill, overlooking a lake below and wooded valley. The drive approaches the side of the building, which is not very imposing, but the white-stone front is attractive.

The château is very much a family home, and Mme Sandrier, a capable and friendly woman, is very easy-going and likes her guests to be happy. There are several public rooms, including a sitting-room with a magnificent Venetian-glass chandelier and some delicate seventeenth-century murals; but these rooms have a rather scruffy look, as though a fresh coat of paint is long overdue. The bedrooms on the first floor are quite palatial; those on the second floor are smaller and simpler. The château is much used by young people, especially those travelling through the Loire on horse-back. It's a friendly and cheerful place to stay.

RAZINES - Richelieu CENTRE - Indre-et-Loire

75 CHATEAU DE MILLY H

⛨ ★★
Razines, 37120 Richelieu,
Indre-et-Loire.
Tel: 47 95 64 56
Propr: Mme Michiko Akiyama
Open: Easter - 31 Oct

Total rooms: 15 B-C

No lift

Restaurant: Open daily
Prix fixe: Menus at A at B
A la carte available
Demi-pension B-C

Seminars: max. 25

Credit cards:
Am Ex, Diners Club
Eurocard, Visa
English spoken

Tennis court 9km
Swimming pool 9km
Horse riding 9km

Châteaux Hôtels Indép.

30km south of Chinon. From there, take the D749, through Richelieu and on a further 9km. The château is on the left of the main road. **Airport:** *Tours (71km)* **Station:** *Tours (69km)*

From the outside, this is an impressive eighteenth-century château set in wooded parkland. Built of grey stone with a white-brick decorative-facing around the windows and doorways, it has at the back a beautiful domed tower, topped with a cupola that dwarfs the nearby trees.

In 1988, a new owner took over this château. Since then, a new staff has been appointed, considerable improvements have already been made and more are planned, including creating additional bedrooms and adding a swimming pool. As a result, the château now has a welcome freshness. Although the bedrooms vary in size, all are comfortable, with good bathrooms. The dining-room is large and inviting. It continues to be very popular with people in the area — a clear sign that the standard of the food is above average.

BEAUMONT-EN-VERON - Avoine CENTRE - Indre-et-Loire

76 MANOIR DE MONTOUR PG

♁♁ ★	Double with shower	2 B	Fishing 1km
Beaumont-en-Veron, 37420	Double with bath	1 B	Swimming 2km
Avoine, Indre-et-Loire.	Total rooms:	3	Tennis court 2km
Tel: 47 58 43 76	+ 2 Apartments		Horse riding 2km
Prop: Mme Krebs			
Open: Easter — 11 Nov	No restaurant		Château Accueil
	No credit cards		Les Etapes Francois Coeur
No lift			

6km west of Chinon. From there, take the D749 towards Bourgueil. After 4km, the road bends sharply to the right. At this point go straight on to Montour. The château is on the left, just before the cross-roads in the village. **Airport:** *Tours (45km)* **Station:** *Port-Boulet (6km)*

First constructed in the seventeenth century and extended in the eighteenth, this agreeable country house was once a silk farm. Now it is very much a family home, where guests are welcome. Although Mme Krebs speaks very little English, she is a most amenable hostess.

Guests are served breakfast at a refectory table in the beamed dining-room. There is also a sitting room with comfortable settees, a huge fireplace and painted wood-panelling. It has a casual but stylish appearance.

From the stone-flagged hall, a wooden staircase leads to a long corridor with its polished floor-boards that seem to lean at a somewhat unnerving angle. The largest and most expensive bedroom is heavily beamed and well furnished. The other two rooms are much smaller. Although the beds in these are very comfortable, the shower and toilet facilities are cramped into a rather confined space.

As no evening meal is served, we drove into Chinon, where a restaurant Au Plaisir Gourmand provides splendid fare that has justifiably been awarded a Michelin rosette. But after eating, we returned to Montour where we wandered along the deserted lanes that led through abundant vineyards. A pleasant, restful experience.

SAINT-EPIAN - Azay-le-Rideau CENTRE - Indre-et-Loire

77 HOSTELLERIE DU CHATEAU DE MONTGOGER H

🛡 ★★★
Saint-Epian, au sud D57, 37800 Azay-le-Rideau.
Tel: 47 65 54 22
Telex: 752 380 F
Propr: Mme Christel & M. Jacques Debat-Cauvin
Open: All year

Twin with bath	9 C-D
Double with bath	3 C-D
Suites (max. 4)	2 D
Total rooms:	14

No lift

Restaurant: Open daily
Cuisine de femme, supervised by Mme Debat-Cauvin.
Prix fixe: Menus at A & B
A la carte available
Demi-pension (2 days+) D-F
Specialities: *Foie gras frais de canard en terrine ou cuisiné chaud; Poissons et gibiers au gré des saisons.*

Seminars: max. 25

Credit cards:
Am Ex, Diners Club
Mastercard, Visa
English & Spanish spoken

Swimming pool
Tennis court
Practice golf
Fishing

Châteaux Hôtels Indép.
Inter. Leading Association

40km south of Tours. From there, take the D751 to Azay-le-Rideau. Turn into the town and cross the Indre. Immediately afterwards, turn left on to the D17 and then take the first right onto the D57 Saint-Epian, where turn left on to the D21. Montgoger is on the right after 1.3km. **Airport:** *Tours (25km)* **Station:** *Tours*

The narrow pot-holed drive winds up a wooded hill past the overgrown ruins of an old château. At the top, surrounded by a grassy meadow, is the Hostellerie. It is a long, low building, with a line of large, arched windows on the ground floor. Once it had been the château's orangery, but it was converted into a house after all but the outer walls of the main building had been destroyed by fire in 1882.

The building is not particularly impressive, but it is attractive and in a delightful and utterly peaceful position. The proprietors have redecorated and refurbished the hotel. All the bedrooms are charming. The dining room, however, has a hectic air about it, with busy patterns on the chairs and carpet. It is a pity, because it is otherwise an elegant room with a beamed ceiling and impressive chandelier. The cuisine, expertly supervised by Mme Debat-Cauvin, is most enjoyable.

78 HOSTELLERIE DU CHATEAU DE ROCHECOTTE H

♔ ★ ★ ★
Saint-Patrice, 37130
Langeais, Indre-et-Loir.
Tel: 47 96 90 62, 47 96 91 28
Propr: the Pasquier family
Open: All year

Twin with bath	9 B-C
Double with bath	10 B-C
Suites	2 C-D
Total rooms:	21

No lift

Restaurant: Open daily
Chef: M. Thierry Marx
Lunch: 1200 - 1330
Dinner: 1930 - 2100
Prix fixe 1 menu at A
A la carte available
Demi-pension (3 days +) C-E
Specialities:*Effeuillé de turbot aux pointes d'asperges et son ragout de petits légumes en feuilleté; Tatin de pigeon aux pommes Roseval et jus de trufle; Hure de lapereau aux fines herbes et sa gelée de Vouvray.*

Seminars: max. 50
Groups: max. 30
Receptions: max. 120
Credit cards:
American Express
Diners Club
Eurocard
English, German & Italian spoken

Fishing 2km
Horse riding 2km
Golf course 15km

Châteaux Hôtels Indép.

30km south-west of Tours. From there, take the N152, along the north bank of the Loire. Turn right on the D35 towards Bourgueil. The château is on the right, in the village of Saint-Patrice. **Airport:** *Tours (32km)* **Station:** *Saint-Patrice (500m)*

Originally called 'Roche sur le coteau' ('Rock on the hill') in the fifteenth century, the château passed through various hands and rebuildings until it was bought in 1825 by the Duchesse de Dino, wife of Talleyrand's nephew. She transformed the château into an Italian villa, adding columns, pergolas and flower-beds. Thus was created the breathtakingly beautiful mansion of classic proportions that stands in a dense forest on the hill overlooking the village of Saint-Patrice.

In the autumn of 1985, M. and Mme Pasquier and their daughters bought the château and set about turning it into a luxurious hotel. Aided by the designer, Christian Belloy, they renovated and decorated the complete interior. Little that is authentic remains, but the soft modern style that has been imposed on the elegant rooms is appealing.

Cream-coloured fabrics with soft pastel patterns and delicate coloured carpets are everywhere. Modern lighting sends warm patterns over the rich cream walls. The dining room is spectacular. The ornate plasterwork on the ceiling has been meticulously repainted; there are huge palms and free standing, amber-pink columns. The whole effect is delicate and charming.

The bedrooms are equally delightful - the same delicate colours have been used and although much of the furniture is modern there are scattered throughout lovely antique pieces. Everywhere is kept luxuriously warm. Even on a cool summer evening, the newly-installed central-heating springs into action - but with disastrous results. After centuries of cold, damp winters, the constant heat has dried out the wood and great cracks have already appeared in the carefully redecorated wood panelling and doors throughout the château.

Although so recently opened, the restaurant has already acquired a good reputation. The chef, Thierry Marx, previously worked at the much-lauded Taillevent in Paris. His cuisine is innovative and his sweets are especially delightful. Enjoy, for example, *Terrine de chocolat double au café brûlot* or *Chaud froid aux cerises et son arôme pistache.* Mouth-watering!

SAVIGNE-SUR-LATHAN CENTRE - Indre-et-Loire

79 CHATEAU DE BEAULIEU PG

⛨ ★
37340 Savigné-sur-Lathan, Indre-et-Loire.
Tel: 47 24 21 21
Propr: Baron & Baronne de Saint-Vaulry
Open: 1 Apr - 4 Nov

No lift

Twin with bath 1 B
Double with bath 1 B
(inc. breakfast)
Total rooms: 2
Table d'hôte on request A

No credit cards
English spoken

Tennis court
Horse riding 8km
Swimming pool 15km

Gîtes de France

30km north west of Tours. The easiest, but slightly longer, route from Tours is to take the N152 along the north bank of the Loire. At Cinq-Mars. turn right on to the D34. After 16.5km tunr left on to the D69. The château is 2km further on the right. **Airport:** *Tours (32km)* **Station:** *Tours (30km)*

A long drive lined with poplars leads to the Château de Beaulieu. Three sides of its vast gravelled courtyard are lined by buildings. Facing the drive is a small wall topped with iron railings and double wrought iron gates. The large central wing was built in the middle of the seventeenth century as a centre for Protestant studies; the two smaller wings were added towards the end of the next century.

The present owners, Baron and Baronne de Saint-Vaulry, are a charming couple who were most anxious to make us welcome and to show us around their home. The rooms downstairs are homely - not at all in the grand style that matches either their spaciousness or the imposing exterior. The largest bedroom, which has a double bed, is elegantly furnished, with a beautiful rug on the polished wood floor. The other room has twin beds and is very simple. Both rooms share a bathroom and w.c.

Although the château is in no way luxurious, it provides an opportunity to spend time with a delightful, warm couple in the peace and tranquillity of the French countryside.

80 CHATEAU DE CHISSAY H

🛡🛡 ★★★
Chissay-en-Touraine, 41400
Montrichard, Loir-et-Cher.
Tel: 54 32 32 01
Telex: 750 393 F
Propr: M. P. Savry, a
Hôtels Particuliers
Direc: M. P. Longet
Open: 1 March - 31 Dec

Twin with shower	10	C-E
Twin with bath	10	C-E
Suites (max. 4)	8	E
Total rooms:	28	

Lift. 1 ground-floor room.

Restaurant: Open daily
Chef: M. Xavier Ancelot
Lunch: 1200 - 1330
Dinner: 1930 - 2130
Prix fixe: Menus at A & B
A la carte available
Demi-pension (3 days+) C-D
Specialities: *Ballotine de foie gras; Aiguillettes de saumon; Turbot marine aux herbes; Compote de lapereau en gelée aux herbes fines; Gigot d'agneau à la tourengelle.*

Seminars: max. 25
Groups: max. 30
Credit cards:
Access
American Express
Visa
English, German, Italian & Spanish spoken

Swimming pool
Horse riding 2km
Tennis courts 4km
Golf course 20km

Relais & Châteaux

37km south-west of Blois. From there, cross the Loire and take the D751. After 10km, the D751 turns off to the left, but continue south on what has become the D764 to Montrichard. There turn left along the north bank of the Cher. At Chissay-en-Touraine, you pass the château on the right. Take the next right and drive up the hill to the hotel entrance. **Airport:** *Tours (38km)* **Station:** *Chissay-en-Touraine*

In a prominent position overlooking the Valley of the Cher, this white-stone château was built in the sixteenth century, although it incorporates the keep from an earlier eleventh-century building. An authentic royal palace, it was owned by both Charles VII and Louis XI. Later it belonged to the Duc de Choiseul, one of Louis XV's ministers. In the summer of 1985 it was opened as the latest in the group of hotels belonging to the Savry family. It still has about it the air of legends. The entrance is through a vaulted stone passage-way which leads into a small courtyard. From its loggia, there is a spectacular view of the valley below. Cars have to be left in the road, but the reception area is by the entrance.

We were impressed by the hotel. The public rooms, including the dining area, have a timeless, soothing atmosphere. The dark tea-rose colour on the walls harmonises well with the wood panelling and old oak furniture. The bedrooms are stylishly plain with lovely furnishings and luxurious bathrooms, slightly marred by an intrusive mosaic.

The position of the château is superb; the grounds are pretty; and the heated swimming pool is a delight. The staff we met were kind and most helpful.

COUDDES - Contres | CENTRE - Loir-et-Cher

81 CHATEAU DE LA BASME PG

♛♛
Couddes, 41700 Contres,
Loir- et-Cher.
Tel: 54 71 32 05
Propr: Mme Marie Magdeleine Dupont-Baranger
Open: All year

Twin with shower 2 A
Twin with bath 1 B
Double with shower 1 A
(inc. breakfast)
Total rooms: 4
(All with shared w.c.)

No lift

No restaurant

No credit cards

Swimming pool 3km
Tennis court 3km

Gîtes de France

26km south of Blois. From there, take the D956 to Contres and then the D675 to Couddes. Turn right into the village and take the road towards Choussy. The château is 3km further on the right. **Airport:** *Blois (35km)* **Station:** *Blois (26km)*

The ancient walls and buildings of this château totally enclose two giant, open squares - one is a gravelled courtyard, the other is a French garden shaded by massive trees. There is a moat, a large round dovecote and some of the buildings are half-timbered. Parts of the château date back to the fifteenth century. Living there in 1515 was Jeanne Chaudrin who on 2 February that year married Louis de Ronsard. She bore him six children, one of whom was Pierre de Ronsard, the poet.

This chateau is an ideal place for French-speaking tourists who wish to enjoy life in a farming community that is remote and yet close to the major tourist attractions of the Loire valley.

FRETEVAL - Morée CENTRE - Loir-et-Cher

82 CHATEAU DE ROCHEUX PG

♛♛★
Fréteval, 41160 Morée,
Loir-et-Cher.
Tel: 54 23 26 80
Proprs: M. & Mme Brugues
Open: All year

Twin with bath	12 B
Double with bath	6 B
Suite (max. 3)	1 C
Total rooms:	19

No lift

Restaurant: Open daily
Prix fixe: 3 menus at A
Lunch: 1200 - 1400
Dinner: 1930 - 2100
Demi-pension (6 days+) B
Specialities: *Souffles aus fruits frais, Canard aux poires, Tarte Tatin.*

Seminars: max. 30
Groups: max. 25
Credit cards:
American Express
Diners Club
Visa
Spanish spoken

Golf course 3km
Tennis court 6km
Swimming pool 6km
Châteaux et Demures de Tradition

18km north-east of Vendôme. From there take the N10 towards Châteaudun. After 11km, at Pezou, turn right across the Loir and turn left on to the D12 through Lignières. The château is 2km further on the left, just before the village of Rocheux. **Airport:** *Blois (20km)* **Station:** *Vendôme (18km)*

Built in 1551 on the site of an older castle, Rocheux was at the beginning of the eighteenth century the home of Marc Hyacinthe de Rosmadec, Viceroy of the Indies and Governor of the French territories in the Americas. Set in extensive wooded grounds of forty-five acres, the brick and stone exterior of this large château is still impressive.

The interior has some interesting features, such as the open fireplace, stained-glass windows and the stone plaques in the beamed dining-room, the carved wooden panelling and the ornate coving in the saloon, and some antique furniture, including a Louis XVI bed and wardrobe. The bedrooms are comfortable and the bathrooms are adequate. The restaurant provides a selection of traditional dishes at reasonable prices.

Although there is a somewhat old-fashioned style about the château, it provides an inexpensive place to stay in a delightful setting, not far from the main tourist centres of the Loire Valley.

HUISSEAU-SUR-COSSON CENTRE - Loir-et-Cher

83 CHATEAU DE NANTEUIL H

⛨⛨ ★
Huisseay-sur-Cosson, 41350
Vineuil, Loir-et-Cher.
Tel: 54 42 61 98
Propr: M. Frédéric Théry
Open: 1 Feb - 31 Dec

Twin - shared w.c.	3	A
Twin with bath	7	A-B
Suites	2	C
Total rooms:	12	

No lift

Restaurant: closed Mon
Chef: M. Pedrono Meilteur
Lunch: 1200 - 1400
Dinner: 1930 - 2100
Prixe fixe: 3 menus at A
Demi-pension (3 days+) B
Specialities: *Escalope de saumon au beurre blanc; Veritable haddock d'ecosse sauce persil; Aiguillette de canard; Glaces et desserts maison.*

Seminars: max. 15
Groups: max. 20
Receptions: max. 150
English & German spoken

Tennis court 6km
Horse riding 6km

Châteaux et Demeures de Tradition

8km west of Blois. From there, take the D956. After crossing the Loir, take the second exit from the dual-carriageway. Cross under it to take the D33 towards Chambord. The château is 3km further on the left. **Airport:** *Tours (50km)* **Station:** *Blois (7km)*

This appealing château stands beside the River Cosson and is mirrored in its smooth waters. Acquired before the First World War by an Englishman, it was turned into a hotel by his grandson, Frédéric Théry, in 1975. With grounds covering seven acres, it is a peaceful and romantic place to stay. The cuisine, although traditional, is prepared imaginatively, with a special emphasis being placed on fish dishes. In fine weather, meals are served on the terrace. With its panelled walls and pleasant furniture, the dining room is, however, a most agreeable place in which to eat. The bedrooms are welcoming and well decorated. All have magnificent views of the River Cosson. The three very cheap rooms with shared W.C. are on the top floor. The other far more commodious rooms are on the floor below. The welcome of the host and the standards of service are above reproach. As the prices of both accommodation and food are so low, this hotel represents one of the best bargains in the Loire valley.

84 CHATEAU DE COLLIERS PG

⚜⚜ ★★
Muides-sur-Loire, 41500 Mer, Loir-et-Cher.
Tel: 54 87 50 75
Props: M. Christian & Mme Marie-France de Gelis
Open: 1 March - 31 Dec (winter on request)

Twin with bath	3 C
Double with bath	1 C
Suite (max. 4)	1 D
(inc. breakfast)	
Total rooms	5

No lift. 2 ground-floor rooms

Table d'hote on request A

No credit cards
Groups: max 12
English & Spanish spoken

Hunting
Tennis court 800m
Swimming pool 5km
Golf course 12km

Château Accueil

17km north-east of Blois. From there, cross to the south bank of the river by the D174. Immediately afterwards, turn left onto the D951 to Montivault (and towards Orleans). 16.5km later (and 2km after the village of Saint-Dye-sur-Loire), the entrance to the château is on the left, just before Muides-sur-Loire. **Airport:** *Chapelle-Vandomois (21km)* **Station:** *Mer (5km)*

As early as the fourteenth century, there was a feudal estate at Colliers. The present château was built at the beginning of the eighteenth century by Jacques Gabriel, the Royal architect, and has subsequently been modified. In 1776, it was bought by Pierre de Rigaud, the Marquis de Vaudreuil, who was the king's lieutenant general in Canada and the Governor of Louisiana. A few years later, the château was acquired by the ancestors of the present owners.

Its position is superb. Not only is it virtually on the south bank of the River Loire, but it is almost in the back-garden of the magnificent Château de Chambord, which is only 5km away.

Very much a family home, Château de Colliers is an elegant and substantial building that is filled with family heirlooms and interesting furnishings. The bedrooms are well equipped and comfortable, with splendid views. An excellent table d'hote is available on request.

Top: **Château de Craon** (44) Mayenne (Pays de la Loire)
Bottom: **Château de Nieuil** (94) Charente (Poitou-Charentes)

Top: **Château du Gue-pean** (85) Loir-et-Cher (Centre)
Bottom: **Château de Montledier** (137) Tarn (Midi-Pyrenees)

MONTHOU-SUR-CHER - Montrichard CENTRE - Loir-et-Cher

85 CHATEAU DU GUE-PEAN PG

♛♛♛ ★
Monthou-sur-Cher, 41400
Montrichard, Loir-et-Cher.
Tel: 54 71 43 01/ 46 09
Telex: 750 382 F
Open: All year
Propr: Marquis de Keguelin

Twin with shower	7 B-C
Double with bath	13 B-C
Suites (max. 5)	2 C
Total rooms:	22

10 bedrooms in the château & 12 in annexe
No lift

Restaurant: open daily
Chef: M. Verron
Lunch: 1300
Dinner: 2045
Prix fixe 1 menu at A
Demi-pension C-D
Specialities: Fresh fish, seasoned game.

Seminars: max. 25
Groups: max. 40
No credit cards
English spoken

Tennis court
Concerts
Exhibitions

Châteaux Hôtels Indép.

33km south of Blois. From there, take the D764 to Pontlevoy, where turn left on the D85 to Monthou-sur-Cher. Turn left through the village. The château is on the right. **Airport:** *Tours (44km)* **Station:** *Blois (33km)*

So much has happened in this much-visited historic monument that it would take a long volume to record even an outline. It was the home of the Valois kings, Francois I, Henri II and Henri III; it has been visited by Louis XII, Charles Brandon Duke of Suffolk, Talleyrand and the Shah of Iran; Balzac wrote Louis Lambert in the library and Chopin, it is said, composed Valse Brillante while a guest there.

Details of every important event that has taken place at Gué-Péan seem to be known to the genial and magisterial proprietor, Marquis de Keguelin, a descendant of the Comtes d'Aprement who took up residence there in 1676.

The château is much older than that. It started life as a hunting lodge and was transformed into a fortified stronghold. An enormous keep leads into an elegant, rectangular court-yard, which is bordered by two Renaissance pavilions in the style of Henri II and two L-shaped wings built in the early part of the seventeenth century. Inside is a storehouse of antiques and relics - Louis XV furniture, tapestries, and paintings by masters, including Andrea del Sarto and David. The library contains a permanent exhibition of autographs. There is also an imposing king's bedroom, where most of the French royal family seem to have slept, including Francois I and his innumerable mistresses.

Of course, the available guest rooms are not so sumptuous - indeed they are somewhat basic and a few share bathrooms. Recent visitors have reported that the grounds were overgrown, outbuildings were neglected and the restaurant was closed.

MONTRICHARD CENTRE - Loir-et-Cher

86 CHATEAU DE LA MENAUDIERE

H

★

B.P.13, 41401 Montrichard
Cedex, Loir-et-Cher.
Tel: 54 32 02 44
Telex: 751 246 F
Open: 1 Mar - 30 Nov
Propr: Mutuelle Generale de l'Education Nationale
Direc: Mme Colette Moulard

Twin with shower	4	B-C
Twin with bath	11	B-C
Double with shopwer	1	B
Double with bath	7	B-C
Single	2	B
Total rooms:	25	

Restaurant: Open daily
Lunch: 1200 - 1330
Dinner: 1900 - 2130
Prix fixe 2 menus at B
A la carte available
Demi-pension (3 days+) C-D
Specialities:*Paupiettes de saumon au caviar; Terrine de foie canard maison; Bar (bass) et saumon fumés au château.*

No lift. 1 ground-floor room.

Seminars: max. 40
Groups: max. 48
Credit cards:
American Express
Diners Club
Eurocard
Mastercard
English & German spoken

Horse riding 2km
Swimming pool 3km
Tennis courts 3km
Fishing 3km

Châteaux Hôtels Indép.

35km south-west of Blois. From there, take the D751 and after 9km, when it branches right, keep straight on along the D764 to Montrichard. Pass through the town and take the D115 towards Amboise. The long drive to the château is 2km further on the right. **Airport:** *Tours (43km)* **Station:** *Montrichard (2km)*

Approached down a long avenue lined with oaks, this château at first appears faceless, like someone seen from behind. However, having passed through an eighteenth-century, towered porch-way, you see the main building across a large courtyard. Originally built in the early part of the fifteenth century, but frequently restored, it lacks the grace and splendour usually found in buildings of that period. In 1981 it was opened as a hotel and restaurant.

Because of its position beside the main road from Amboise to Montrichard, La Menaudière is busy and the staff, though helpful, seem a mite harassed. The bedrooms vary in size - none are notable, although all are comfortable and have good bathrooms. The two dining rooms are the most attractive areas.

ONZAIN CENTRE - Loir-et-Cher

87 DOMAINE DES HAUTS-DE-LOIRE H

🛡🛡 ★★★
Route d'Herbault, 41150
Onzain, Loir-et-Cher.
Tel: 54 20 72 57
Telex: 751 547 F
Open: 1 Mar - 30 Nov
Propr: M. Gaston & Mme Janine Bonnigal
Direc: M. Pierre-Alain Bon nigal

Twin with bath	13	C-E
Double with bath	9	E
Suites	5	F-H
Total rooms:	27	

No lift. 4 ground-floor rooms.

Restaurant: Open daily
Chef: M. G. Hummel
Lunch: 1215 - 1415
Dinner: 1915 - 2115
Prix fixe: 2 menus at B
A la carte available
Specialities: *Mousse de persil à l'huile de noisettes; Filet de sandre* (pike-like fish) *à El'orange*

Seminars: max. 40
Groups: max. 30
Credit cards:
American Express
Diners Club
Eurocard
Visa
English & German spoken

Tennis court
Swimming pool 5km
Horse riding 13km
Golf 38km

Relais & Châteaux

21km south-west of Blois. From there, take the N152. After 16km, opposite the bridge to Chaumont-sur-Loire, turn right. Pass through Onzain and take the road to Herbault. The château is a further 3km. **Airport:** *Tours (45km)* **Station:** *Onzain (3km)*

There are many things that make Le Domaine des Hauts-de-Loire special. The park of over sixty-five acres is part of an ancient, tranquil forest. Swans swim on the large pond in the flower-filled garden at the front of the house. The chef, Gerard Hummel, is talented and inspired - his cuisine boasts a Michelin rosette. But best of all is the the quality of the interior, for it has the feel of a luxurious home that has been in the same family for centuries. Yet it was less than twenty years ago that the Bonnigals purchased the house which, despite its feeling of age, was not built until the 1860s. In the 1880s, a subsequent owner made considerable additions, doubling the size of the main building and adding an orangerie, conservatories, stables, and servants' quarters.

Throughout the interior, the Bonnigals have with real flair selected fine furniture from different periods which harmonise well with their settings. The bedrooms are splendid and the bathrooms excellent. The atmosphere and quality of Hauts-de-Loire are exceptional.

The Bonnigal family also owns the successful Hostellerie du Château at Chaumont-sur-Loire.

ONZAIN CENTRE - Loir-et-Cher

88 HOTEL CHATEAU DES TERTRES

H

♁ ★
Route de Montreux, 41150
Onzain, Loir-et-Cher.
Tel: 54 20 83 88
Open: Easter to 11 Nov
Propr: M. Paul Valois

No lift

Twin with bath	9 B
Double with bath	9 B
Total rooms:	18
Apartments:	2

No restaurant

Credit cards:
American Express
Mastercard
Visa
English & German spoken

Tennis court 2km
Fishing 3km
Horse riding 3km

Château Hôtels Indép.

20km south-west of Blois. From there, take the N152. After 16km, opposite the bridge to Chaumont-sur-Loire, turn right. In Onzain, turn left on the D58 towards Monteaux. **Airport.** *Tours (43km)* **Station:** *Onzain (1km)*

Built during the nineteenth century in a small park containing many varieties of trees and carpeted with wild cyclamen, this solid creeper-covered château is an unpretentious and inexpensive family-run hotel. Although there is much heavy furniture and dark wood-panelling of the period, the interior has been pleasantly decorated. For guests, there is a well-furnished sitting-room and beside it a dining-room where breakfast is served. Although varying in size and decorations, the bedrooms are all comfortable.

M. and Mme Valois warmly welcome guests and their château offers a quiet place to stay in a busy tourist area.

RILLY-SUR-LOIRE - Onzain CENTRE - Loir-et-Cher

89 CHATEAU DE LA HAUTE BORDE H

🛡 ★
Rilly-sur-Loire, 41150
Onzain, Loir-et-Cher.
Tel: 54 20 98 09
Propr: M. Very
Open: 1 Feb - 15 Dec

Twin with shower	2 A
Twin with bath	3 B
Double with shower	5 A
Double with bath	2 B
Suite (max. 4)	1 B
Double with bidet	5 A
Total rooms:	18

No lift. 2 ground-floor rooms.

Restaurant: Closed Sun eves and Mons
Chef: M. Very
Lunch: 1230 - 1345
Dinner: 1930 - 2045
Prix fixe: 3 menus at A
A la carte available
Demi-pension (3 days+) A-B
Specialities: *Souffle de coquilles Saint Jacque; Canard a l'orange.*

Seminars: max. 25
Groups: max. 30

Credit cards:
Eurocard
Visa

Tennis court 5km
Swimming pool 5km
Horse riding 13km

29km south-west of Blois on the south bank of the Loire. After crossing, take the D751. The château is mid-way between the villages of Chaumont and Rilly-sur-Loire on the right. **Airport:** *Tours (43km)* **Station:** *Onzain (5km)*

This is a large, attractive, white-stone château with a square crenellated tower at the front. The large grounds border the Loire. Owned by the same family for several generations, it is run as a simple, unprepossessing hotel. Popular with French families, it is simple, clean, comfortable, and very inexpensive.

TROO - Montoire-sur-le-Loir CENTRE - Loir-et-Cher

90 CHATEAU DE LA VOUTE PG

⛉⛉ ★
Troo, 41800 Montoire-sur-le-Loir, Loir-et-Cher.
Tel: 54 72 52 52
Prop: M.J. Clays
Direcs: M.J. Clays & M.C. Venon
Open: All year

Twin with shower	1 B
Twin with bath	1 C
Double with bath	1 C
Suites (max. 4)	2 B-C
Total rooms	5

No lift

No restaurant

Credit cards:
American Express
Visa
English spoken

Swimming pool 5km
Tennis courts 5km

52km north of Tours. 6km west of Montoire-sur-le-Loir. From there, take the D917 to the village of Troo. The entrance to the château is on the left. **Airport:** *Tours (49km)* **Station:** *Vendôme (25km)*

The ancient keep, originally built on this site, was captured in 1188 by the army of Richard the Lion-heart. The present, elegant château, with its stone walls and grey slate roof, was constructed in the sixteenth century and considerably modified during the eighteenth. In its early days, the château had many royal associations. In 1551, Henri II visited Diane de Poitiers there. A decade later, Antoine de Bourbon lived in the château, as, in 1562, at the outbreak of the religious wars, did the young Henri de Navare, the future Henri IV.

In 1987, the château was acquired by the present owners. Both are antique-dealers and their carefully renovated home is now furnished with charming period pieces and paintings. Each of the bedrooms has been given a name which its style reflects, such as Pompadour, Louis XIII and Empire. It is a château with style and character. As it borders the gentle Loir, it also offers delightful views of a part of this river valley famed for its rural tranquility.

Although without a restaurant, the château provides an ideal base for exploring the area. Troo itself is an interesting village with a maze of narrow streets and galleries that are partially dug into the side of a hill. It also boasts a twelfth-century church, a fossil cave and the Puits-Qui-Parle, or echoing well.

LA FERTE-SAINT-AUBIN CENTRE - Loiret

91 CHATEAU LES MUIDS H

🛡 ★★
RN 20, 45240 La Ferté-Saint-Aubin, Loiret.
Tel: 38 64 65 14
Fax: 38 76 50 08
Propr: SARL Loisir Mediterranee
Dir: M.J.G. Rochette
Open: 1 Feb - 15 Jan
Total rooms: 23 B-C (13 are in the château and 10 in a new annexe)
No lift. 2 ground-floor rooms.

Restaurant: Open daily
Chef: M. Christian Monange
Lunch: 1200 - 1400
Dinner: 1900 - 2200
Prix fixe: Menus at A & B
A la carte available
Specialities. *Foie gras chaud au caramel de poir; Consommé de langoustines en croûte; Dos de carpe au vin rouge; Carré de chevreuil; Canette aux deux cuissons; Nougat glacé.*

Seminars: max. 30
Receptions: max 60
Credit cards:
American Express
Diners Club
Visa
English & German spoken

Fishing
Tennis court 2km
Swimming pool 2km
Horse riding 10km
Golf course 10km
La Castellerie

25km south of Orleans. From there, take the N20 through La Ferté-Saint-Aubin. The château is a further 5km on the right. **Airport:** *Orleans (32km)* **Station:** *La Ferté-Saint-Aubin (5km)*

The exterior of this château is impressive. Built at the end of the eighteenth century, it seems to copy on a grand-scale much earlier fortifications. At the front, there is a large central section with a square tower at one end and a turreted wing at the other. Smaller crenellated wings and square towers complete the square. On the facade, there are geometrical patterns in red and grey brick and an ornamented entrance. Many of the windows have white-painted shutters. Seen from across the reflecting lake, the château is magnificent.

In 1989, under new management, a considerable number of changes were made to the château. Most inportant of these was the addition of 10 bedrooms in a new annexe. Those in the château itself are spacious, well equipped and comfortable. The public rooms, with their low ceilings, wooden panelling and parquet floors are typical of the late nineteenth century. The cuisine is good, with a varied menu that includes regional specialities. Set in a vast wooded park of over sixty acres, Les Muids is a pleasant and popular place to stay in an unspoilt area, known as the Sologne.

92 DOMAINE DE CHICAMOUR H

★★

Sury-aux-Bois, 45530 Vitry-aux-Loges, Loiret.
Tel: 38 59 35 42
Props: M. Robert & Mme A. Merckx
Open: 1 March - 30 Nov

Double with shower	9 B
Double with bath	3 B
Total rooms	12

No lift

Restaurant: Open daily
Lunch: 1215 - 1330
Dinner: 1930 - 2100
Prix fixe: 3 menus at A
A la carte available
Demi-pension (min. 2 days) B
Specialities: *Foie de canard frais, Saint-Jacques et qruenelles de saumon au beurre blanc, Poêlon de poire.*

Seminars: max. 50
Groups: max. 24
Credit cards:
Eurocard
Visa
English, German & Dutch spoken

Horse-riding
Hunting
Fishing
Tennis courts
Golf course 20km

Relais du Silence

11km north-east of Châteauneuf-sur-Loire. From there, take the N60 towards Bellegarde. After 11km, the entrance to the château is on the right. **Airport:** *Saint-Denis-en-Val (15km)* **Station:** *Orleans (35km).*

In a park of 18 acres and surrounded by the vast Forest of Orleans, this neat three-storeyed château was originally constructed in 1833. It has been transformed into a hotel that is simple, comfortable and friendly. There is a homely lounge with deep settees and a large fireplace. In the pleasant restaurant, a variety of regional dishes are served, using locally-grown produce. The bedrooms, like the bathrooms, are well equipped. All have a superb view across the park.

In the grounds, there is a tennis club and an equitation centre that can be used by guests staying at the hotel. Between October and May, it is also possible to join in a hunt. During the rest of the year, the guests — and deer — can wander at their leisure through the eighty thousand acres of surrounding forest.

Domaine de Chicamour provides a peaceful retreat, just a few miles away from the valley of the Loire.

MONTBRON POITOU-CHARENTES - Charente

93 CHATEAU SAINTE-CATHERINE H

♡ ★
Route Departementale 16,
16220 Montbron, Charente.
Tel: 45 23 60 03
Propr: Mme Monique Chupin
Open: 1 Feb - 31 Dec
Twin with shower 5 A-B
Twin with bath 7 B-C
Double with shower 1 B
Double with bath 5 B-C
Total rooms: 18

Restaurant: Open daily
Chef: M. Thierry Verrat
Lunch: 1200 - 1400
Dinner: 1930 - 2130
Prix fixe: Menus at A & B
A la carte available
Demi-pension (5 days+) B-C
Specialities: *Coquelet sauce champagne; Rognons perigourdins.*

No lift

Seminars: max. 30
Groups: max. 30
Receptions: max. 100
Credit cards: All.
English spoken

Swimming pool
Tennis court 3km
Horse riding 3km
Golf course 25km
Relais du Silence
Châteaux Hôtels Indép.

26km east of Angoulême. From there, take the D939. After 7km, turn left on to the D4. At Marthon, turn left on to the D16. The château is 4km further on the right. **Airport:** *Angoulême (28km)* **Station:** *Angoulême (26km)*

We were expecting a lot from this château. It is set amongst marvellous rolling countryside and it has interesting historical associations. Built in the seventeenth century, it passed through various hands until, after the French Revolution, it was purchased by Louis Benjamin du Rousseau de Ferrieres. He was unfortunate enough to be a friend of the beautiful scheming Empress Josephine, wife of Napoleon. She persuaded poor Louis to search for her missing niece in Martinique. In gratitude, while he was away, the Empress turned up at his house and ordered the building of two tall wings at either end of the original château. The work was carried out quickly. The Empress returned to Paris, forgetting to pay the builders. Napoleon, a dutiful husband, had to settle the account.

It is the interior of the château that disappoints. Immediately on entering, the visitor is confronted with a blue, green and brown swirling-patterned carpet, heavily-patterned turquoise wallpaper, and a vast arrangement of multi-coloured plastic flowers. In the bedrooms, in addition to vivid floral wallpaper, there are nylon leopard-skin covers and framed prints of galloping horses and lurid sunsets.

The dining room is very pleasant, and staff are enthusiastic and helpful.

NIEUEIL POITOU-CHARENTES - Charente

94 CHATEAU DE NIEUIL H

⛨⛨★★★
16270, Nieuil, Charente.
Tel: 45 71 36 38
Telex: 791 230 F
Propr: M. Jean-Michel Bodinaud
Open: 1 Mar - 12 Nov

Double with bath	12	C-D
Suites	3	D-F
Total rooms:	15	

No lift. 2 ground-floor rooms and ramps.

Restaurant: Closed Wed lunch, except for guests
Chef: Mme Luce Bodinaud
Prix fixe: Menus at A & B
A la carte available
Specialities: *Cassolette d'huîtes à la crème d'échalotes; Fricassée de poulet au cognac; Sauté d'agneau à la fondue de tomate; Farci charentais.*

Credit cards:
American Express
Diners Club
Visa
English spoken

Art gallery
Fishing
Swimming pool
Tennis court

Relais & Châteaux

45km north-east of Angoulême. From there, take the D941 (joining the N141) through La Rochefoucauld. After 42km, turn left on the D739 towards Nieuil. **Airport:** *Angoulême (39km)* **Station:** *Chasseneui (11km)*

This beautiful and palatial château was built as a hunting-lodge in the early part of the sixteenth century by Francois I at about the time he was also constructing a masterpiece of the Renaissance, the Château de Chambord. Discovering that an Englishman, called Grunn, owned a parcel of land within the royal estate at Chambord, Francois I offered to exchange it for Nieuil - a bargain the Englishman gladly accepted.

Eventually the white-stone château with its towers, a wide moat and a wooded park of over 350 acres, was acquired by the Bodinaud family. In 1889, it was partially restored and then, in 1937, an historic event took place. Jean-Michel's grandfather opened Nieuil as the very first château-hôtel in France.

The interior is as exquisite as the exterior. There is an impressive marble staircase, vast Gothic fireplaces, tooled cordoba leather friezes and dark oak panelling. All the bedrooms are given aristocratic names - Marquis, Vicomtesse, Princesse. Mme Bodinaud, who used to lecture on design, has employed her

considerable talents in decorating with sophisticated taste all the rooms, which are furnished with antiques, Aubusson tapestries and beautiful paintings. She is also the chef and has acquired an excellent reputation - her cuisine has been awarded a Michelin rosette. As well as being an affable host, her husband, Jean-Michel, is also an art enthusiast. One of the stables has been converted into a gallery where prints and paintings are exhibited and sold.

At the back of the house, there is a formal French garden and on the other side of a row of trees the swimming pool, where a cold buffet lunch is served. In the extensive grounds, there are chestnut groves, a hazel wood and a lake full of fish. Château de Nieuil is a delightful place to stay.

SAINT-FORT-SUR-GIRONDE POITOU-CHARENTES - Charente-Maritime

95 CHATEAU DES SALLES PG

🛡🛡 ★
17240 Saint-Fort-sur-Gironde.
Charente-Maritime.
Tel: 46 49 95 10
Propr: Mme Thèsy & M. Jean Couillaud
Open: Easter - 30 Sep

Twin with shower	1 B
Twin with bath	1 B
Double with shower	3 B
Suite (max. 5)	1 C
Total rooms:	6

No lift

Table d'hôte (res only) A
Lunch: 1230
Dinner: 2000
Demi-pension (4 days+) B
Specialities: *Charcuterie* (cooked pork) *et patisserie maison;* Fresh fish from Gironde estuary.

Credit cards:
Eurocard
Mastercard
Visa
English spoken

Tennis courts 1.5km
Sea 2km
Horse Riding 15km
Châteaux et Demeures de Tradition
Les Etapes Francois Coeur
Châteaux Hôtels Indép.

32km south-east of Royan. From there, take the D730 through Cozes. The private drive to the château is a further 15km on the right. **Airport:** *Saintes (33km)* **Station:** *Jonzac (33km) or Saintes*

This toy-fort of a château was built in 1863 by Charles Henri De Pont in the style of the twelfth century, complete with an enclosed courtyard, towers and machicolations. Close to the estuary of the River Gironde and in the midst of woods and farmland, it is a pretty, tranquil spot. The château has its own vineyard and M. and Mme Couillaud, the owners, produce wine, Cognac and the excellent fortified wine, Pineau des Charentes, which is made from must (unfermented grape juice) and Cognac. The Couillands have totally restored their château and make guests very welcome in their delightful, friendly and informal home.

USSEAU - Mauze-sur-le-Mignon POITOU-CHARENTES - Deux-Sèvres

96 CHATEAU D'OLBREUSE H

🛡 ★★
Usseau, 79210 Mauze-sur-le-Mignon, Deux-Sèvres.
Tel: 49 04 85 74
Propr: M. & Mme Maingueneau
Direc: M. & Mme Arrivé
Open: 1 Mar - 31 Jan, except 1st week in Oct.

Twin with shower	2 A-B
Twin with bath	3 B
Double with shower	1 B
Double with bath	5 B
Total rooms:	11

No lift. 4 ground-floor rooms, 1 equipped for the handicapped.

Restaurant: Closed Sun eves & Mons except in high season
Chef: M. Jean Arrivé
Lunch: 1200 - 1400
Dinner: 1930 - 2100
Prix fixe: Menus at A & B
A la carte available
Demi-pension (3 days+) B
Specialities: *Magret de canard au chèvre; Ris de veau braisés au pineau; Nougat glacé à l'Angelique de Niort; Sabayon au cidre.*

Seminars: max. 30
Groups: max. 20
Receptions: max. 200
Credit cards: Visa

Tennis court 2km
Swimming pool 6km
Horse riding 16km
Golf course 20km

Châteaux Hôtels Indép.

24km south-west of Niort. From there, take the N11. After 14km leave the dual carriageway at Epannes and take the D115 towards Usseau. After 3km, at La Rochenard, turn right on the road to Olbreuse. **Airport:** *La Rochelle (47km)* **Station:** *Mauze (8km)*

The present owners can trace their family back to the Desmiers, who originally built the Château d'Olbreuse at the beginning of the thirteenth century. Eléonore Desmier d'Olbreuse married Georges-William of Brunswick-Celle and their daughter, Sophie-Dorothée, was the mother of George II of England. Olbreuse was given by George II to a cousin of Eléonore, Alexander Prévost de Gagemont. The last of his descendants died in 1870 and the property reverted to Charles Desmier d'Olbreuse. His grand-daughter, Christiane, and her husband, Felix Maingueneau, restored the château and opened it as a hotel.

Everywhere is furnished simply. Exposed brick and stone-work abounds, looking fine in the ancient kitchen but slightly bleak elsewhere. The bedrooms are pleasant and some have four-poster beds. The restaurant is very popular locally - the food is good, the prices are very reasonable, and the desserts are splendid.

BRUX - Civray POITOU-CHARENTES - Vienne

97 CHATEAU D'EPANVILLIERS PG

🛡🛡🛡 ★
Brux, 86400 Civray, Vienne.
Tel: 49 67 18 43
Propr: M. Jean-Robert Lorzil
Open: Weekends and school holidays

Double with bath 2 C

No lift

No restaurant
No credit cards

English spoken

Horse riding 7km
Swimming pool 10km
Tennis court 10km

Gîtes de France

46km south of Poitiers. From there, take the N10 to Couhé, where turn off and enter the town, continuing towards Civray on the D7. The château is up a long track on the right, just before reaching the village of Epanvilliers. **Airport:** *Poitiers (48km)* **Station:** *Vivonne (26km) or Poitiers*

A remarkable man has, almost single-handed, restored this château which, when he purchased it over a decade ago, was derelict and roofless. While continuing to work as a teacher, Jean-Robert Lorzil has spent all his spare moments and every cent he could raise painstakingly and lovingly giving back to his château the life and grandeur it had once possessed.

Originally built at the end of the seventeenth century, the château was totally renovated about 1750, making it an elegant residence with an imposing classical facade. During the French Revolution, about fifty priests were hidden there by the Marquis d'Epanvilliers. As the building was ransacked and damaged, the château was barely habitable by the time the Marquis died in 1825.

Now every room has been restored to its eighteenth century splendour, filled with furniture, paintings and objects of the period. Some of these belonged to Jean-Robert Lorzil's family. When the Second World War broke out, his parents removed all the precious furniture from their château in the north of France and concealed it in various places. It was just as well, because their château was destroyed in the bombing. Other pieces come from museums, because the regional government was so impressed by the work that Jean-Robert had done that they asked him if he would be willing to open his château as a living museum, where children could come and stay for a week to learn about and understand aspects

of their country's history. Now, during the school term, some forty or so pupils spend a week at a time staying and working at the château. They sleep in outbuildings that have been converted into dormitories. The château is also open to the public every afternoon, except Thursdays.

When we arrived at the château, we found ourselves caught up in a guided tour. It was rather odd, afterwards, to step over the white rope and sit down to tea amongst what had been, a few minutes earlier, the exhibits. The guest bedrooms are also peeped into during the tour - if they're empty. And they are amazing. One has a four-poster bed set in an alcove. There is a narrow gap between the bed and the wall and a minute hole in the partition wall so that the person on that side of the bed can get up without disturbing the sleeping-partner.

Because of the limited times that the two guest-rooms are available, it is essential to make a reservation. It's well worth it!

CELLE-L'EVESCAULT - Lusignan POITOU-CHARENTES - Vienne

98 CHATEAU DE LA LIVRAIE PG

Celle-l'Evescault, 86600
Lusignan, Vienne.
Tel: 49 43 52 59
Propr: M. René & Mme Eva Morin
Open: All year

No lift

Twin with shower 3 A
Twin with bath 1 A
Double with shower 3 B
Double with bath 1 B
(inc. breakfast)
Total rooms: 8
Apartment: 1

Table d'hôte (res only) A
Dinner: 1900 - 2100
Demi-pension B

No credit cards
Groups: max. 10

Stabling
Fishing 3km
Swimming 3km
Tennis court 3km

Gîtes de France

22km south-west of Poitiers. From there, take the N10. At Vivonne, turn right on to the D742 towards Lusignan. After 7km, turn left on the tiny D97 towards Les Minières. (Note that at this junction Celle L'Evescault is off to the right. Don't go that way.) Take the second on the right (a further 3km). It leads to the château. **Airport:** *Poitiers (24km)* **Station:** *Vivonne (10km)*

It's almost worth going to Château de la Livraie just for the drive along the maze of tiny country lanes meandering through lush rolling countryside.

A large grey-stoned building, La Livraie has the air of a farm-house rather than a château - and that indeed is what it is. M. Morin keeps flocks of sheep and cattle on his land. Mme Morin ushers visitors straight into her massive kitchen, which seems to have a fire always ablaze in the enormous fireplace. In front of it is a giant refectory table, covered with a plastic gingham tablecloth. Modern teak-finish kitchen-units vie with ancient wallpaper. This is where breakfast and the evening meal are served. Asked to describe her food, Mme Morin said it was 'Cuisine à la table familiale dans un cadre de verdure en milieu rural.' Exactly. There's no nouvelle cuisine here - nor any miniscule portions. It's good, honest farmhouse cooking, using the fresh vegetables from the garden. It's also one of the cheapest meals available in France.

Upstairs, the bedrooms are comfortable and unpretentious. Several of them do not have their own w.c. A real taste of rural France.

---

99 CHATEAU DE PERIGNY H

⛨★★★
Perigny, 86190 Vouillé,
Vienne.
Tel: 49 51 80 43
Telex: 791 400 F
Fax: 49 51 90 09
Propr: M. Egon Dideriksen
Direcs: M. Eric & Mme Annie Perrot
Open 1 March - 30 Nov

Single with shower	1	B
Double with shower	3	B
Twin with bath	19	C-D
Double with bath	16	B-D
Suites	3	E
Total rooms:	42	

Lift. 9 ground-floor rooms.

Restaurant: Open daily
Chef: M. Claude Gautier
Lunch: 1215 - 1345
Dinner: 1915 - 2130
Prix fixe: Menus at A & B
A la carte available
Demi-pension (3 days+) D-G
Specialities: *Saumon cru mariné à la danoise; Escalope de sandre au Gamay du Haut-Poitou; Filet de morue aux aromates; Feuillantine de ris de veau aux échalotes.*

Seminars: max. 100
Groups: max. 70
Receptions: max. 250
Credit cards:
American Express
Diners Club
Visa
English, Danish & Spanish spoken

Swimming pool
Tennis courts
Horse riding
Golf course 20km

Châteaux Hôtels Indép.
Relais du Silence

15km from Poitiers. From there, take the N149 towards Nantes. After 15km, turn left along the narrow D43. The château is down a long drive on the left. **Airport:** *Poitiers (12km)* **Station:** *Poitiers (14km).*

After a period of decline, this well-known hotel was acquired in 1988 by a Danish businessman, M. Egon Dideriksen, who has reversed the unfortunate trend with a comprehensive restyling. Much of the interior has been redecorated and refurbished. The restaurant is bright and uncluttered, with crisp white tablecloths and an attractive display of pot-plants and flowers.

Many of the bedrooms and all the public rooms are not in the château, but in a large square of connected stone-buildings that have been modernised. A short distance away is the tall, grey-stone, turreted château which contains the more expensive bedrooms. Under the new regime, these have been greatly improved. All the bathrooms have been redecorated; two luxurious suites have been created

on the third floor, and a comfortable sitting room has been added on the ground floor.

M. Dideriksen has appointed new staff, including the chef and the efficient couple who are the managers. The cuisine has been highly praised and Château de Perigny has again become a pleasurable place to eat.

Located in a delightful park, overlooking a pretty valley and only a twenty-minute drive away from Poitiers, the hotel provides a delightful and peaceful hide-away which, after the many changes made by the new owner, is beginning to recover its former glory.

SERIGNY POITOU-CHARENTES - Vienne

100 CHATEAU DE SAINT-BONNET

PG

★★	Twin with shower 2 C	No credit cards
86230 Sérigny, Vienne.	Twin with bath 1 D	English & Spanish spoken
Tel: 45 77 62 27, 49 86 01 55	Double with shower 2 C	
Propr: M. Maurice & Mme Nicole Vivant	Total rooms: 5	Horse riding 2km Tennis court 10km
Open: 1 Jun - 30 Sep	Table d'hôte - Saturdays A	Swimming pool 10km
No lift	Groups: max. 10	Châteaux Hôtels Indép. Les Etapes Francois Coeur

30km south of Chinon. From there, take the D749 through Richelieu. 4km afterwards, turn right on to the D757 towards Lencloître. After 11km, turn right on to the tiny D66. Cross over a junction and the château is a little further on the right. **Airport:** *Poitiers (45km)* **Station:** *Châtellerault (25km)*

With gleaming white stone walls and shiny new slates atop the corner towers, this pretty, small, squat château sits in a perfectly-maintained garden with the air of a new architect-designed home. In fact it dates from the fifteenth century, although in recent years Maurice and Nicole Vivant (who are both Parisian designers) have lavished time and money on completely renovating and modernising the château, which is their summer home. As a result, everything is pristine and there is no feel of being in an old family home.

The house, however, has some splendid features and the rooms are all bright and cheerful, although the wallpapers may not be to everyone's taste. The bedrooms are fresh and comfortable. Each is decorated in a different style - Spanish and American colonial among them. The best have old beds and crocheted white cotton bed-spreads. The bathrooms are above reproach. Any guest can be confident of a warm welcome, efficient service and an enjoyable stay.

101 CHATEAU DE TERNAY PG

♡♡♡ ★
Ternay, 86120 Les Trois Moutiers, Vienne.
Tel: 49 22 92 82, 41 87 56 85
Propr: Marquis & Marquise de Ternay
Open: All year

No lift

Twin with bath 1 C
Double with bath 1 C
(inc. breakfast)
Total rooms: 2
Table d'hôte (res only) A
(inc. aperitif & wine)

No credit cards
English spoken

Tennis court 7km
Swimming pool 10km
Golf course 25km

Les Etapes Francois Coeur
Gîtes de France

30km south-west of Chinon. From there, take the D749 across the River Vienne and then turn right on the D751. At the first junction, turn left on to the D759. Shortly afterwards, turn right towards Thouars. 4.5km after Les Trois Moutiers, turn right on the D14 to Ternay. The château is on the right at the entrance to the village. **Airport:** Poitiers (67km) **Station:** *Loudun (11km)*

This is a place you'll either love or hate. If you're looking for push-button hotel service, this château is not for you; but if you want a comfortable stay in an unrestored, spectacular castle, this is the place for it. Ternay started as a twelfth-century fortified tower that was restored three hundred years later. At that time, there was also built a round tower and a beautiful Gothic chapel. In the seventeenth century, two wings were added, so that now a quadrangle of buildings encloses a central courtyard. The whole lot was renovated in 1883 and given a new facade. Not much has been done since then and the château is certainly showing signs of age and neglect, but it is still spectacular, with vaulted ceilings, covered walks and wonderful antiques. In contrast to much of the rest, the two guest bedrooms are beautifully decorated and perfectly furnished. There is an old four-poster bed in one, and two lovely high beds with hanging drapes in the other. Guests also have use of a drawing room, a games room, a billiard room and a lounge.

Marquis de Ternay breeds goats, and cheese is made at the château. A stay at Ternay is a rare and interesting experience.

---

102 CASTEL NOVEL H

🛡🛡★★★
Route d'Objat, 19240 Varetz, Corrèze.
Tel: 55 85 00 01
Telex: 590 065 F
Fax: 55 85 09 03
Propr: M. Albert Parveaux
Open: 1 May - 16 Oct

Twin with bath	24	C-E
Double with bath	8	C-E
Suites	5	E-G
Total rooms:	37	

(10 in annexe, 50m away)

Lift

Restaurant: Open daily
Chef: M. Jean Pierre Faucher
Lunch: 1200 - 1400
Dinner: 1930 - 2100
Prix fixe: Menus at A & B
A la carte available
Demi-pension C-E
Specialities: *Foie gras de canard en terrine; Tourtière de pintadeau aux salsifis* (young guinea-fowl in a pie with oyster-plant).

Seminars: max. 60
Groups: max. 60
Credit cards:
American Express
Diners Club
Visa
English, German & Spanish spoken

Swimming pool
Tennis court
Practice golf
Horse riding 10km

Relais & Châteaux

10km north-east of Brive-la-Gaillarde. From there, take the D901 to Varetz, where turn left to the château. **Airport:** *Brive (8km)* **Station:** *Brive (10km)*

The Parveaux family have been running hotels for over a century and they certainly know what they're doing. Having for some years run a successful hotel at the Alpine ski resort of Courchevel, M. Parveaux senior set about transforming into a luxury hotel this ivy-covered, grey turreted castle which has stood high above the Vezere valley since the beginning of the Middle Ages. Now managed by his son, Albert, and his daughter-in-law, Christine, Château de Castel Novel is a hotel of distinction. In the early part of this century, the château was owned by Henri de Jouvenal, the erstwhile French Ambassador in Rome, whose wife was the famous novelist, Colette. At that time, many famous people stayed at Castel Novel. They still do - the names in the guest-book include the late David Niven and Jacques Chirac.

The Parveaux family also own and operate as a hotel the Château de Puy Robert (q.v.). Both have a special feel and style. With pleated fabric festooned on the ceilings of some bedrooms, a mixture of antique and ultra-modern furniture, gilt-painted beams and canopied four-posters, the decor could well be over the top. But it isn't. It is dragged back from the edge by sensitive choice of delicate fabrics, plain carpets in strong colours, and beautiful arrangements of flowers. The difficult task of being striking without being over-cluttered and complex has been satisfactorily achieved.

There is much to please the discerning guest - especially the cuisine. Richly deserving the Michelin rosette, the food of Jean Pierre Faucher is the best of Périgourdian dishes, all beautifully presented - foie gras, truffles, veal and delicious mushrooms. There are also many excellent regional wines (Bergerac and Cahors).

103 CHATEAU MOUNET-SULLY H

★	Twin with bath	4 B	Groups: max. 8
Route de Mussidan, 24100 Bergerac, Dordogne.	Double with bath	4 B	Credit cards: American Express, Diners Club, Visa
Tel: 53 57 04 21	Total rooms:	8	
Propr: M. Christian Lonvaud	No lift		
Direc: M. Laurent Pesterbe	No restaurant		English & Italian spoken
Open: 1 Jun - 15 Oct			

2.5km north-east of Bergerac on the D709 to Mussidan. **Airport:** *Bergerac (6km)* **Station:** *Bergerac (3km)*

This château was built towards the end of the last century for Mounet-Sully, the famous French actor who was an intimate friend of Sarah Bernhardt. He commanded that the building should not be a copy of any special architectural style. It turned out to be a disconcerting mixture of them all - medieval, Gothic, Florentine and Roman. What looks a little like a modern office block is topped with half-timbered watch-towers; butting on to it is a low-slung building with dormer windows and a long verandah; there are Italianate columns and sculptures. Inside is even more kitsch. Frescoes abound to glorify the owner, including one in the salon showing him in a passionate embrace with Sarah Bernhardt - a scene, it is said, that was often re-enacted there. His crowning aggrandisement was a large private theatre in the grounds.

What glory there was in the place is now somewhat faded. The bedrooms are rather bleak and wild plants threaten to take over the covered walks. It is, however, very popular locally and many wedding receptions and disco dances are held there.

104 CHATEAU RAULY-SAULIEUT H

♁♁★★
24240 Monbazillac, Dordogne.
Tel: 53 63 35 31
Proprs: M. César Kientzy &
M. Lionel Craveski
Open: 1 Feb - 31 Dec

Twin with bath	4 C
Double with bath	4 C
Suite	1 E
Total rooms	9

No lift

Restaurant: Closed Mon, except in high season
Prix fixe: Menus at A & B
A la carte available
Demi-pension: B-C
Specialities: *Flan de cèpes au coulis de tomates fraîches, Foie gras à la gelée de Monbazillac, Tourte de canard aux pleurotes et aux truffes.*

Seminars: max. 50
Groups: max. 12
Credit cards:
American Express
Diners Card
Visa

Swimming pool
Tennis courts at 1km
Horse riding at 5km
Golf course at 10km
Châteaux Hôtels Indép.

7km south-west of Bergerac. From there, take the D933 towards Eymet. After 5km, turn right onto the D14. The entrance to the châteaux is a further 2km on the right. **Airport:** *Bergerac (6km)* **Station:** *Bergerac (7km)*

Nestling among hillside vineyards and set in an extensive parkland of ancient woods and landscaped gardens, the château is a most welcome addition to this guide. Completed around 1860 in an uncommon architectural style, called Chartreuse Bordelaise, it is an elegant, symmetrical country house, built of mellowed white stone and roofed with grey tiles.

Renovated and refurbished with great care and sensitivity, the interior is very attractive and has an authentic air. Some of the bedrooms have oriental rugs on polished floorboards; others are fully carpeted. All are spacious, extremely comfortable and furnished with antiques and interesting objets d'art. All provide spectacular views across the valley of the Dordogne. The bathrooms are excellent.

There are large terracotta-coloured tiles on the floor and stone walls in downstairs rooms, including the pleasant and popular restaurant with its blue and white plates and curtains. The food is most agreeable. Although, sensibly, the choice of dishes is limited, there is still a most interesting mixture of regional and traditional French cuisine. In summer, guests can also dine on the terrace.

The owners' welcome is warm and the service excellent. Strongly recommended.

MONTERRAUD - Beaumont AQUITAINE - Dordogne

105 CHATEAU DE REGAGNAC PG

♥♥♥ ★ ♆
Monterraud, 24440
Beaumont, Dordogne.
Tel: 53 22 42 98 (09.00-12.00)
Propr: M. Serge & Mme Veronique Pardoux
Open: 1 Mar - 31 Jan

Twin with shower	3 B
Twin with bath	1 B
Double with bath	1 B
Total rooms:	5

No lift

Table d'hôte (res only) B (inc. aperitif & wine)
Chef: Mme Veronique Pardoux
Specialities: *Foie gras; Truite; Saumonnie; Aiguillettes de canard.*

Seminars: max. 15
Groups: max. 10

No credit cards
English & Spanish spoken

Tennis court
Fishing 500m
Golf course 15km

This is not the easiest place to find. It is 60km south of Périgueux. From there, take the N89. After 7km, take the D710 to Le Bugue, where cross over the Vézère on the D31E (which after 7km becomes the D51) to Le Buisson. Take the D25 to Cadouin, where turn left on the narrow D2 towards Boulegue. 5km later (having passed two small roads off to the left and then one to the right), turn left where the road forks and then take the next left. It is a track that winds down through a forest and after over 1km reaches the château. **Airport:** *Bergerac (44km)* **Station:** *Le Buisson (12km)*

This ancient walled fortress is planted on a hill overlooking what was the main trade-route to Spain. It still contains a thirteenth-century tower, a fifteenth-century house, an ancient kitchen and a museum of hunting. To the right of the gateway are stables and other interesting outbuildings. In front, across the lawn where peacocks strut disdainfully, is a walled terrace with an imposing view stretching over a vast forest to the distant azure horizon.

The door in the tower opens into a stone-floored hall with a spiralling stone staircase. Beyond is the remarkable dining room which is like a medieval grand-hall. The ceiling is beamed and at the far end is an enormous stone fireplace with all the irons to roast a sheep. Filling much of the room is an old oak refectory table.

It is here that Veronique, Serge Pardoux's delightful oriental wife, serves her famed traditional French suppers, which are far better quality and value than is to be had in many much vaunted restaurants. Using vegetables, fruits and herbs she has grown herself, Mme Pardoux produces regular culinary masterpieces. The menu changes nightly, but one included delicate mushroom soup, slices of ham that had been buried in ashes for a year, trout fried in fresh almonds and cashews, filet of duck, a delightful salad and a cream of chestnut dessert. Three carefully selected wines were also served.

Château de Régagnac, which Serge Pardoux purchased in 1964, is a perfect setting for his unusual collections of memorabilia. There are souvenirs from when he served during the Second World War with the Free French Army and later with the British commandos; impressive displays of rifles, medieval armour, and lead soldiers. Every room is furnished with antiques - canopied beds, beautiful chests, and even a wheel-chair made for Louis XVIII. All the bedrooms are charming - three are in the main building, but the two most delightful ones (called the Duchess and the Spanish) are in an outbuilding.

M. and Mme Pardeux treat all their guests as friends. Their extraordinary home has a rare, intangibly serene quality. It is a most satisfying place to stay - unless you hate dogs or remote rural hideaways.

MONTIGNAC AQUITAINE - Dordogne

106 CHATEAU DE PUY-ROBERT H

⛨ ★★★
24290 Montignac, Dordogne.
Tel: 53 51 92 13
Telex: 550 616 F
Propr: M. Albert Parveaux
Direc: M. P. Moncharmont
Open: 6 May - 15 Oct

Double with bath 36 C-E
Suites 2 E
Total rooms: 38
(15 rooms in the château. 23 rooms in an annexe.)
Lift in château. 6 ground-floor rooms in annexe.

Restaurant: Open daily
Chef: M. Philippe Barthelemy
Lunch: 1200 - 1400
Dinner: 1930 - 2100
Prix fixe: Menus at A & B
A la carte available
Demi-pension C-E
Specialities: *Foie gras frais de canard mi-cuit en terrine; Chausson aux truffes. Brick de turbot aux pailletes d'algues.*

Seminars: max. 30
Groups: max. 50
Credit cards:
American Express
Diners Club
Visa
English, German & Spanish spoken

Swimming pool
Close to Grottes de Lascaux

Relais et Châteaux

2km south-west of Montignac. From there, take a small road beside the river - the D65 towards Valojoux. The château is on the left. **Airport:** *Brive (35km)* **Station:** *Brive (35km)*

Puy-Robert was opened as a hotel in 1986. Like Castel Novel (q.v.), it is owned by the Parveaux family and is decorated and furnished in a similar lavish way by Christine Parveaux. Each of the bedrooms is very different. Not all the decorations will be loved by everybody. We found, for example, that the luminous yellow Monet room was anything but relaxing. The plain white of the palatial bathrooms (complete with magnifying mirrors and hair-driers) was something of a relief. But the overall attention to detail and the exceptionally high standards of luxury and comfort will be widely appreciated.

The dining room is very pretty, with delicate pastel colours - pinks, peaches and blues. The ceiling of the central area is swathed in pleated blue fabric; the Italian chandeliers are decorated with pink and green and blue enamel. The cuisine of the chef, Philippe Barthelemy, has attracted much praise and a Michelin rosette.

The château was built in the middle of the nineteenth century and is a square white-stone building. The new annexe is close-by. They are both unexceptional,

but the location is splendid. Atop a wooded hill, they overlook the beautiful Vezere valley. Within easy walking distance are the famous Lascaux caves with their magnificent prehistoric paintings. (Only an exact replica is now open to the public.)

The young staff at the hotel are most helpful and enthusiastic. (Like Castel Novel, Château Puy-Robert is twinned with a hotel run by the Parveaux family in the ski-resort of Courchevel to which all the staff move during the winter.)

RAZAC-SUR-L'ISLE AQUITAINE - Dordogne

107 CHATEAU DE LALANDE H

★
24430 Razac-sur-l'Isle, Dordogne.
Tel: 53 54 52 30
Propr: M. Bertojo & M. Sicard
Open: 15 Mar - 15 Nov

Double with bath	19 B
Double - shared w.c.	3 B
Total rooms:	22

No lift

Restaurant: Closed Wed except in high season
Lunch: 1230 - 1330
Dinner: 1900 - 2100
Prix fixe: Menus at A & B
A la carte available
Demi-pension B
Specialities: Pork & duck conserves; Duck fillet; Norway lobster gratin; Scallop with vermouth.

Seminars: max. 30
Groups: max. 40
Credit cards:
American Express
Diners Club
Eurocard
Visa

Horse riding 3km
Swimming pool
Tennis courts 10km

10km east of Périgueux. From there, take the D170 along the north bank of the River Isle. After 4.5km, when the road bends sharply to the right, keep straight on, taking the D3 towards Saint-Astair. The entrance to the château is a further 5km on the left. **Airport:** *Périgueux (16km)* **Station:** *Périgueux (10km)*

Built in the eighteenth century and much extended in the nineteenth, Château de Lalande is set on a hill amidst a small wooded park. It is a hotel with a rather pleasant, old-fashioned air. M. and Mme Sicard are a jolly couple who are patient and helpful with foreign guests. The decorations are unremarkable, but inoffensive. Everywhere has the appearance of a genteel pre-war boarding-house on the English south-coast. The bedrooms on the first floors are of a good size and some have old pieces of furniture. The rooms on the second floor are smaller, but quite comfortable. The lounge and dining room are bright and pleasant. The restaurant is popular and the food is traditional, adequate and inexpensive. There is nothing particularly exceptional about this hotel - but it's clean, convenient and cheap.

108 CHATEAU DE ROGNAC H

♥ ★
Rognac, 24330 Bassilac,
Dordogne.
Tel: 53 54 40 78
Propr: Mme Daudrix
Open: Easter - 31 October

Double with shower	4	A
Double with bath	8	B
Total rooms:	12	

No lift

Restaurant: Open daily
Prix fixe: 2 menus at A
Demi-pension (3 days+) B-C

No credit cards

Beside river
Tennis courts 6km

8km west of Périgueux. From there, take the N21 through Trelissac. Take the next right at Charieras and by a narrow bridge cross the River Isle. Immediately afterwards, there is a junction. Do not go towards Bassilac, but take the left turn around the airport to Rognac. The château is down by the river. **Airport:** *Périgueux Bassilac (1km)* **Station:** *Périgueux (9km)*

Perched alongside, and in places overhanging, the River Isle, this round-turreted stone château was first built in the sixteenth century. When the present owner, Mme Daudrix, inherited it in 1963, it was in ruins. She and her husband undertook the formidable task of restoration and conversion into a hotel.

Mme Daudrix is a great character, full of joie de vivre and most entertaining company. As well as running the hotel and the bar, she seems to do all the cooking - her restaurant is very popular in the area for good country fare.

There is nothing sophisticated about this château. The interior is dark with high stone walls and beamed ceilings. There is a large dining room and a small but comfortable lounge and bar-area with a giant television-set. The bedrooms are simple, but adequate. Each room has an extra bed that can be used for a small supplementary payment. There are fantastic views over the river and countryside beyond. It is a very informal, inexpensive and delightfully French hotel.

Top: **Château de Regagnac** (105) Dordogne (Aquitaine)
Bottom: **Château du Crozillat** (126) Haute-Garonne (Midi-Pyrenees)

Château de Lalande (107) Dordogne (Aquitaine)

VEYRIGNAC - Carlux | AQUITAINE - Dordogne

109 CHATEAU DE VEYRIGNAC PG

♛♛ ★★
Veyrignac, 24370 Carlux, Dordogne.
Tel: 53 28 13 56
Propr: M. Geoffrey Kenyon-May
Open: 1 Feb - 21 Dec

Twin with shower	5 C
Double with shower	2 C
Total rooms:	7

Apartments: 3 (in cottages)
No lift

Table d'hôte (res. only) A
Chef: Mme Kenyon-May
Dinner: 20.00
Demi-pension (3 days+) B
Specialities: *Fois gras, Magret de canard; Confit.*

Seminars: max. 20
Groups: max. 15

Credit cards:
American Express
Diners Club
English & Spanish spoken

Swimming pool
Tennis court
By the Dordogne
Hunting & fishing

Les Etapes Francois Coeur

Châteaux Hôtels Indép.

14km south-west of Sarlat-la-Canegal. From there, take the D704. Just after crossing the Dordogne, turn right to Veyrignac. In the village, turn left opposite the church. The narrow lane passes a couple of houses and leads to the château. **Airport:** *Périgueux (75km)* **Station:** *Sarlat (14km)*

Château de Veyrignac is owned by one of those Englishmen who can turn his hand to anything. He and his French wife are excellent hosts and entertaining company. Their home was built in the thirteenth century as a monastery - as a result the ground-floor rooms are vaulted. In the seventeenth century, it was taken over by the Marquis de Cahor, who transformed it into a château. During the Second World War it was used as a headquarters by the Resistance, but when this was discovered by the German army it was burned down. Reroofed and partially restored in 1958, it was acquired by Geoffrey Kenyon-May in 1986 and he has since completed the restoration.

Standing in lovely grounds that drop down to the River Dordogne, the large and elegant yellow-stone château has a slight air of faded grandeur. A notice on the front door advises visitors to bang hard. When they do, the echo reverberates noisily around the vast entrance hall. Inside is light and bright, with a flagstone floor, stone walls and a sweeping flight of stone stairs with a wrought-iron balustrade. The sitting room is large yet intimate, with cosy, well-used furniture, an enormous fireplace and views across the Dordogne Valley. The vaulted dining room is delightful. Mme Kenyon-May is a good cook and food is often grilled on the vast open fire. Sitting with the convivial company round the long refectory table in the glow of candlelight and with the fire casting flickering shadows on the stone walls and ceiling is a memorable experience. The bedrooms are all tastefully decorated and with interesting furniture - some of the wonderful beds were bought from a nearby convent!

This is a very relaxed place that provides an excellent base for exploring the Dordogne. The Kenyon-Mays will do as much or as little as their guests wish. If required, they provide an escorted, six-day tour of the area. In the summer, there are regular balloon flights over the spectacular countryside. Inside the châteaux there are several permanent exhibitions. A museum of armour and a salle de torture are located in a thirteenth-century cellar. In the old chapel, there is a display of historic personalities in period costume. For the visitors who want only to relax, there is a swimming pool and a fifty-acre estate along the banks of the Dordogne.

110 HOSTELLERIE DU CHATEAU DE ROLLAND H

★

R.N. 113, Barsac, 33720 Podensac, Gironde.
Tel: 56 27 15 75, 56 27 19 20
Propr: Mme Anne Duvillie
Open: All year (by reservation in winter)

Twin with bath	7 B	
Double with bath	3 C	
Total rooms:	10	

No lift

Restaurant: Closed Wed in winter
Chef: M. Eric Delteil
Lunch: 1230 - 1430
Dinner: 2000 - 2200
Prix fixe: Menus at A & B
A la carte available
Specialities: *Terrine de foie de canard;* Kidneys cooked in Sauterne; Duck conserves.

Seminars: max. 25
Groups: max. 20
Receptions: max. 40
Credit cards:
American Express
Diners Club
Visa
English spoken

Fishing

Châteaux Hôtels Indép.
La Castellerie

38km south-east of Bordeaux. From there, take the N113 and turn right into the village of Barsac. **Airport:** *Bordeaux Merignac (43km)* **Station:** *Langon (8km)*

There is little to show that this building was a monastery in the fifteenth century. Now it looks what it is — a small hotel with a popular restaurant. You can't miss the place - its name is blazoned on its white walls in Gothic script. There are only ten rooms, which are unpretentious and comfortable. The major feature of the château is the restaurant. It is a charming room with a heavily beamed ceiling, stone fireplace and a tiled floor. The food produced by the chef, Eric Delteil, is splendid and very popular locally. He uses traditional recipes and fresh local produce. His pastries are excellent. The château is a pleasing place to eat and a convenient overnight stop, only 4km away from exit 2 on Autoroute 62.

111 CHATEAU D'ARBIEU PG

♥ ★★
33430 Bazas, Gironde.
Tel: 56 25 11 18
Propr: Comte & Comtesse
Philippe de Chènerilles.
Open: All year
(reservations in winter)

No lift

Table d'hôte (res. only) A
Dinner: 2000

Credit cards: Visa
English spoken

Swimming pool
Tennis court 1km
Horse riding 1km

Château Accueil
Gîtes de France

Double with shower	2 B
Suite (max. 4)	1 C
(inc. breakfast)	
Total rooms:	3

15km south of Langon (and exit 3 of Autoroute 62). From there, take the D952 and after 12km turn left into Bazas. The château is 1km further on the D655 to Casteljaloux. **Airport:** *Bordeaux/Mérignac (71km)* **Station:** *Langon (14km)*

In the heart of the Bazas region, near the Sauterne vineyards, this is one of the newest châteaux in France. Originally built in the nineteenth century, it was gutted by a fire in 1963 that destroyed everything apart from most of the furniture and two rooms. It was rebuilt with one floor less than the original. Its new gleaming-white facade and russet tiles are set against the green background of ancient trees. With modern plumbing and antique furniture, the château has something of the best of both worlds. But perhaps the most interesting feature of a stay is sharing the evening meal with the Comte and Comtesse, although, as they speak only a little English, you'll enjoy it more if you speak some French.

112 CHATEAU DE CAMIAC ET SAINT-DENIS H

★★
33420 Camiac et Saint-Denis, Gironde.
Tel: 56 23 20 85
Propr: M. Bertheau
Open: 1 Apr - 15 Dec

Twin with bath	2 B
Double with bath	11 B
Suites	4 C
Total rooms:	17

No lift. 1 ground-floor room.

No restaurant

Seminars: max. 25
Groups: max. 30
No credit cards

Swimming pool
Tennis court
Billiard room

25km from Bordeaux. From there, take the D936 towards Bergerac. After 20km, turn right on the D20 towards Creon. The château is a further 5km on the right. **Airport:** *Bordeaux/Mérignac (28km)* **Station:** *Creon (3km)*

The château was constructed in 1830. In 1982, it was converted into a modern hotel. The white-stone, three-storeyed building has a tower at each corner and looks quite impressive. The interior, however, has nothing - apart from the odd stone wall - to show that the building has any history. Everything is new and modern - the furniture, the windows, and all the fixtures and fittings. There are sunken circular baths, pine-panelled ceilings and headboards, open staircases, and potted plants everywhere. Catering largely for receptions and business meetings, the hotel nevertheless provides first-class accommodation and facilities which happen to be in a nineteenth-century château.

SAINT-ANDRE-DU-BOIS - Saint-Macaire AQUITAINE - Gironde

113 CHATEAU MALROME H

♛♛♛ ★
Saint-André-du-Bois, 33490
Saint-Macaire, Gironde.
Tel: 56 63 74 92
Propr: M. André Sagne
Direc: Mlle Nicole Cazemajour
Open: All year

No lift

Twin with shower	3 B-C
Twin with bath	1 C
Double with shower	2 C
Suite (max. 3)	1 D
Total rooms:	7

Table d'hôte on reservation (Sunday lunch only) B

Seminars: max. 50
Groups: max. 15
Receptions: max. 200
No credit cards

Tennis court 8km
Swimming pool 8km
Horse riding 8km
Châteaux Hôtels Indép.
Les Etapes Francois Coeur

49km south-east of Bordeaux. From there, take the D10. Just after Sainte-Croix-du-Mont, turn left on the D120 to Verdelais. Take the third right, which leads to the D19. There turn left. After 1km, the road forks. Take the right road (D19E5). The château is on the left. **Airport:** *Bordeaux/Mérignac (60km)* **Station:** *Langon (8km)*

Malromé was the family home of the painter, Toulouse Lautrec. It was there that he died on 9 September 1901.

His mother, Comtesse Adele de Toulouse Lautrec Monja, bought the château in 1885 and renovated the buildings that had been originally constructed between the twelfth and fifteenth centuries. Set among vineyards, the ancient stone buildings form an enormous square around a central courtyard.

The spectacular interior has recently been completely and meticulously restored. The wooden floors are highly polished, the magnificent Renaissance fireplaces gleam, the ornate beams in the ceilings have been cleaned and the decoration regilded. There is period furniture throughout, much of it having belonged to the Lautrec family. From mid-June to mid-September and every Sunday, the château is open during the afternoons to the public. And there is much to see, including the bedrooms of both Henri de Toulouse-Lautrec and his mother. The château is much used for such festivities as weddings and cocktail parties. Wine is also sold.

It is a fascinating place to visit or in which to stay although the guest rooms are simpler and much smaller than those open to the public. The staff do not speak English, but give everyone a warm welcome.

---

114 CHATEAU DE COMMARQUE PG

⛉ ★★
Sauternes, 33210 Langon, Gironde.
Tel: hotel - 56 63 65 94
restaurant - 56 63 68 08
Propr: Dr Nigel & Mme Georgia Reay-Jones
Open: 10 Mar - 10 Jan

Twin and shower	1 A
Suites (max. 4)	5 B
Duples (for 3)	1 B
Total rooms:	7

Restaurant: Open daily
Chef: M. Gilles Couzon
Lunch: 1200 - 1400
Dinner: 1930 - 2200
Prix fixe: 3 menus at A
A la carte available
Demi-pension (4 days+) B
Specialities: *Cailles au Sauternes, Gigot d'agneau braise au fumet de cepes, Escalope de saumon au vin du château.*
No lift. Suites are on ground floor.

Seminars: max. 15
Groups max. 20
Credit cards:
Access
Mastercard
Visa
English spoken

Swimming pool

6km west of Langon and exit 3 on Autoroute 62. From there, take the D8 to Sauternes. Then follow the signs to the château. **Airport:** *Bordeaux/Mérignac (56km)* **Station:** *Langon (6km)*

Run by an English couple with five children, who took over in July 1966, this château is one of the oldest buildings in Sauternes. It is set in about thirty acres of ground, some of which are planted with vines — the vineyard having the right to the Appellation Contrôlée 'Sauternes'. Before moving to France, Nigel Reay-Jones imported wines from the area into Britain. Since settling there, he's taken to wine-making with enthusiasm. He now sells Sauternes and a dry white wine, fermented *en barrique.* A new chai (wine-house) had been constructed and the old one has been converted into a successful restaurant, which specialises in regional dishes.

The rooms in the château are all small suites that are pleasant and comfortable. As each takes up to four people and as there is a swimming pool and ample grounds, the château is an ideal place for people with children.

The owners do everything they can to help guests, whether they just want a relaxing holiday or to explore the area. Nigel Reay-Jones organises wine-tours. Accompanied trips can be arranged.

GABARRET AQUITAINE - Landes

115 CHATEAU DE BUROS H

★ ★
40310 Gabarret, Landes.
Tel: 58 44 34 30
Propr: M. Jean Durand
Open 1 April - 30 Oct

Twin with bath	5 B
Double with bath	12 B
Suite (max. 4)	1 D
(inc. breakfast)	
Total rooms:	18

No lift. 2 ground-floor rooms.

Restaurant: Closed Wed in low season
Lunch: 1200 - 1400
Dinner: 1900 - 2100
Prix fixe: Menus at A & B
Demi-pension (3 days+) B
Specialities: *Grenadins de lotte à l'orange; Salade de cailles chaudes confites; Foie gras frais; Magret de canard aux fruits de saison; Salmis de palombes; Pâtisserie.*

Seminars: max. 50
Groups: max. 35
Receptions: max. 100
Credit cards:
American Express
Diners Club
Visa
English, Italian & Spanish spoken

Swimming pool
Tennis court

Relais du Silence

68km south-west of Agen (and exit 7 of Autoroute 62). From Agen, take the D656 to Nérac where at a T-junction turn right and then first left on to the D656. The entrance to the château is 34km further on the right - 3km before Gabarret. **Airport:** *Agen (65km)* **Station:** *Agen (69km)*

Built in 1889, this square white-stone château with corner towers has been turned into a simple, pleasant hotel. At night its facade is illuminated and, with its three dining rooms accommodating up to 180 people, it is a popular local place to eat and celebrate. The bedrooms are rather small, but pleasantly and simply decorated, clean and comfortable. The food is straightforward, unpretentious and reasonably priced. The château is set in a wooded park amidst open countryside.

SOUSTONS AQUITAINE - Landes

116 CHATEAU BERGERON H

★★
Rue du Vicomte, 40140
Soustons, Landes.
Tel: 58 41 58 14
Propr: M. Pierre Clavier
Open: 1 Jun - 30 Sep

Twin with bath	7 B
Double with bath	9 B
Total rooms:	16

No lift

Restaurant: Open daily - residents only
Dinner: 1930 - 2100
Prix fixe 2 menus at A
A la carte available
Demi-pension (3 days+) B
Specialities: *Foie gras des landes; Confit et magret de canard; Asperges de soustons; Jambon de Bayonne.*

Seminars: max. 30
Groups: max. 30
Credit cards:
American Express
Visa
English & Spanish spoken

Swimming pool
Tennis courts 1km
Horse riding 2km
Sea 7km
Golf course 15km

42km north-east of Biarritz. 25km west of Dax. From there, the easiest way is to leave by the N124 towards Biarritz and just afterwards turn right on to the D16 to Magesq, where, having passed under the N10, turn left and then right on to the D116 to Soustons. The château is close to the church. **Airport:** *Biarritz (42km)* **Station:** *Dax (25km)*

Standing in the middle of the village, this square house was built of white stone at the end of the nineteenth century. It is set in a small, pretty garden with a pleasant terrace and a bower beside a small stream. There is also a private swimming pool. Although called a 'château', it has no pretentions to grandeur - its charm lies in its simplicity. Its most interesting architectural feature is the black and rose marble fireplaces from the period of Napoleon III in two of the salons.

In the thirties, Château Bergeron sheltered Spanish Republicans and in 1940 it was requisitioned by German troops. After the war, the owner turned it into a simple and friendly hotel.

The restaurant is reserved exclusively for hotel guests and serves regional specialities that are very good value. Open only during the summer season, it provides an agreeable and inexpensive place to stay in a non-frenetic holiday-village, close to a vast lake and only 7km from the Atlantic coast.

MONCLAR D'AGENAIS AQUITAINE - Lot-et-Garonne

117 CHATEAU LA SEIGLAL PG

🛡 ★
47380 Monclar d'Agenais, Lot-et-Garonne.
Tel: 53 41 81 30
Propr: M. & Mme Decourty
Open: All year

No lift

Double with bath 1 A
Double - shared w.c. 3 A
(inc. breakfast)
Total rooms: 4
Table d'hôte (res. only) A
Dinner: 20.00
Demi-pension B

No credit cards

Swimming pool
Fishing
Tennis 2km
Horse riding 10km

Gîtes de France

35km east of exit 6 on Autoroute 62; and 16km west of Villeneuve-sur-Lot, from where take the D911. At Sainte-Livrade turn right on to the D687. After 5.5km do not take the right turn to Monclar, but continue along the D687, taking the next small road on the right. The château is on the left. **Airport:** *Agen (48km)* **Station:** *Villeneuve (16km)*

This is a beautiful and almost unknown area of France. Perched on a promontory, the decaying, medieval village of Monclar d'Agenais is a sleepy place with spectacular views of the surrounding countryside. Nestled at the foot of the hill and surrounded by trees is Le Seiglal, a substantial farm-house built in the middle of the nineteenth century by an architect, Evariste Francois Malbec. It still contains some of his remarkable embellishments, including several ornate fireplaces, that have an idiosyncratic style which seems unlikely ever again to be fashionable.

Vines are growing up its grey-stone walls. The shutters are closed at many of the windows. The place looks rather uninviting. However, there is the warmest of welcomes from the charming and amusing owners, M. and Mme Decourty.

It is very much a family home. The dining room is part of the kitchen and the meals are eaten with the family. And splendid meals they are too - the best of French farmhouse cooking with gigantic servings at half the price of the entrée in many restaurants. Stone stairs lead to a vast landing, off which are the bedrooms. They are basic with an incongruous mixture of old and new decorations - a bedroom with pretty cabbage-rose wallpaper on one wall and cork tiles on another. There is a large pond in the garden and the nights are full of the constant croaking of frogs. La Seiglal is an unpretentious, totally relaxing place to stay.

AGEN-BOÉ AQUITAINE - Lot-et-Garonne

118 CHATEAU SAINT-MARCEL H

★★

Route de Toulouse (RN 113), 47550 Agen-Boé, Lot-et-Garonne.
Tel: 53 96 61 30
Telex: 573 113F
Propr: M. Jean Albani
Open: 1 March - 31 Jan

Twin with bath	22 C-D
Double with bath	1 D
Suites	2 D
Total rooms	25

No lift

Restaurant: Closed Sun dinner & Mondays
Chef: M. Bernard LaFuente
Prixe fixe: 3 menus at A
A la carte available
Demi-pension B-D
Specialities: *Mille feuille de saumon fumé et sa chantilly à la moutarde de Meaux, Pigeonneau rôti aux airelles et riz sauvage, Filet mignon de boeuf aux appétits et petits céréales.*

Seminars: max. 60
Groups: max. 40
Credit cards:
American Express
Diners Club
Visa

Swimming Pool
Tennis court
Golf course 5km

Châteaux Hôtels Indép.
La Castellerie
Inter. Leading Association

10km north-east of exit 7 on Autoroute 62. 8km east of Agen. From there, take the N113. The magnificent cedar-lined drive to the château is on the right. **Airport:** *Agen (10km)* **Station:** *Agen (8km)*

Once the home of the Comte de Montesquieu, this finely proportioned seventeenth-century château with its four turreted, square towers at the corners looks out onto a large cobbled courtyard with a central fountain.

In 1987, the complete building was renovated and refurbished. Now it is a first-class hotel, incorporating both old and new styles. Fifteen of the bedrooms appear very modern. Another eight, which are more spacious, have fine furnishings and are decorated in carefully selected and matching hues — one with pale blues and white, another with soft brown and a deep green. All the bedrooms have modern facilities, including 15-channel television and superb bathrooms. The restaurant has already achieved a fine reputation and presents a variety of menus at reasonable prices. The excellent dining-room has a terrace which overlooks the garden.

Although only a few miles away from the autoroute and even closer to the busy N113, the château is set in a peaceful park of over eight acres that is bordered by the River Garonne.

AGEN-SAINT-NICOLAS DE LA BALERME AQUITANE - Lot-et-Garonne

119 CHATEAU SAINT-PHILIP H

♛♛ ★★
Agen-Saint-Nicolas de la Balerme, 47220 Astaffort, Lot-et- Garonne.
Tel: 53 87 31 73
Propr: Mme Jacqueline & M. René Dupont
Open: All year

Single with bath	2 B
Twin with bath	7 B
Double with bath	2 B
Suite	1 C-D
Total rooms:	12

Restaurant: Open daily
Lunch: 1200 - 1330
Dinner: 1930 - 2130
Prix fixe: Menus at A & B
A la carte available
Demi-pension C

Specialities: *Foie gras chaud de canard à la liqueur de noix, Nougat glacé à la menthe.*

No lift. 1 ground-floor room.

Seminars: max. 70
Groups: max. 18
Credit cards:
American Express
Diners Club
Visa
English spoken

Tennis court
Fishing
Golf course 2km

Châteaux Hôtels Indép.

13km north-west of exit 8 on Autoroute 62. 13km east of Agen. From there, take the N113. After 12km, turn right on the narrow D114 towards Saint-Nicolas. After the second bridge over the river (a single-track, rather rickety suspension bridge!), turn right. The entrance is at the rear right-hand corner. **Airport:** *Agen (19km)* **Station:** *Agen (15km)*

Despite being only a couple of miles from the streaming traffic of the A62 and the N113, this is a peaceful, idyllic spot, right on the south bank of the River Garonne. The original château was built in the late fifteenth century. In the nineteenth century, two rectangular wings were added to the ends of the existing building. Now covered in ivy, the exterior of the château is pleasingly matured.

In 1986, Saint-Philip was purchased by Mme Jacqueline Dupont, who has systematically redecorated the château. The bedrooms are well-furnished - some have four-poster beds and pretty antique furniture. From the two attractive dining rooms there are lovely views over the well-kept garden and the River Garonne. There is an enormous lounge. Far more cosy is the splendid library with its white painted bookcases and gallery. Throughout the château, there are vases of fresh flowers and interesting paintings. Mme Dupont is anxious to perfect her hotel and she is always helpful and considerate. A splendid place to stay and very good value.

120 CASTEL FERRON H

★
Route de Marmande, 47400
Tonneins, Lot-et-Garonne.
Tel: 53 84 59 99
Propr: M. Hermier
Open: All year

Double with bath 17 B-C
No lift

Restaurant: Open daily
Lunch: 1200 - 1430
Dinner: 1930 - 2130
Prix fixe: 4 menus at A

Groups: max. 30
Receptions: max. 200

Credit cards:
American Express
Diners Club
Visa

Swimming pool 1km
Tennis courts 1km
Horse riding 10km

To the west of the N113, 1km north of Tonneins and 18km from exit 6 on Autoroute A62.
Airport: *Agen (44km)* **Station:** *Tonneins (1km)*

The staff are friendly and hospitable; the cuisine is honest and inexpensive; and the château is just off a main highway. The building dates from the fifteeenth century, but there is little evidence of this on the inside, which is decorated using twentieth century materials in a fashion that is perhaps not entirely sympathetic with the age of the château. The furniture is more bland than unattractive. From the terrace outside there are pleasant views. It is not the place for a long stay, but it makes an acceptable overnight stop.

ANGLET AQUITAINE - Pyrénées-Atlantiques

121 CHATEAU DE BRINDOS H

★★
64600 Anglet, Pyrénées-Atlantiques.
Tel: 59 23 17 68
Telex: 541 428 F
Propr: M. Michel & Mme Marie-Pierre Vivensang
Open: All year

Double with bath	13 D-E
Suites	2 F
Total rooms:	15

No lift. 4 ground-floor rooms.

Restaurant: Closed Mons
A la carte only
Specialities: *Foie gras; Grande assiette de la mer; 'Aumelette' à la mode d'Antan.*

Credit cards:
American Express
Diners Club
Visa
English spoken

Swimming pool
Tennis court
Fishing
Sea 3km

Relais & Châteaux

On the outskirts of Biarritz and 3km from Autoroute 63. Take exit 4 for Biarritz and turn right on to the N10. There is a right-turn, just before the airport, to Brindos. **Airport:** *Biarritz (1km)* **Station:** *Biarritz (4km)*

The restaurant of this hotel is one of only three in the extremely popular Biarritz area to have been awarded a Michelin rosette. Because of this, and its pleasant position next to a lake in a rural area that is still within earshot of the town, autoroute and airport, the hotel is extremely popular.

The château was built in the style of a Spanish castle for an Englishman, Reginald Wright, and his American girl-friend, Virginia Gould, in 1920. The public rooms are heavily panelled and beamed. There is a mock-medieval hall with a vast stone fireplace and a galleried corridor. At the outbreak of the Second World War, the Wrights returned to America and their house and its contents were sold.

In 1968, Michel and Marie-Pierre Vivensang purchased the château and embarked on its restoration. Now it is furnished in an opulent, florid style, with richly patterned wallpaper, carpets and upholstery. The bedrooms are less distinctive, though they are large and comfortable. The most memorable has a canopied four-poster bed. There are romantic views over the extensive lake, with its elegant swans and water-lilies.

Although the food is good, only à la carte dishes are available.

BIARRITZ AQUITAINE - Pyrénées-Atlantiques

122 CHATEAU DU CLAIR DE LUNE

♛♛★
48 Avenue Alan Seeger, Route d'Arbonne, 64200, Biarritz, Pyrénées-Atlantiques.
Tel: 59 23 45 96
Propr: M. Dany Beyrière
Open: All year

No lift

Twin with bath	5	B-C
Double with bath	5	B-C
Suites (max. 4)	2	C-D
Total rooms:	12	

No restaurant

Groups: max. 18

Credit cards:
American Express
Diners Club
Visa
English & Spanish spoken
Tennis court 3km
Swimming 3km
Golf course 3km

Château Hôtels Indép.

2km from Autoroute 63. Leave at exit 4 for Biarritz. Turn right on the N10. Before the fly-over, take the lane to Biarritz and then the first right - the D255. The château is on the right. **Airport:** *Biarritz (2km)* **Station:** *Biarritz (4km)*

Biarritz, once an elegant and exclusive resort, gains much of its atmosphere from the elaborate homes built for the wealthy around the turn of the century. One such mansion is Château du Clair de Lune. Set in 16 acres of carefully-tended grounds, the château has delightful views of both the the bay and the distant Pyrenees. It was built in 1902 for M. de Bonand and the American, Miss Anne Harrisson, who later became his wife. It appears to have changed little. Each room is interesting, with delightful details such as huge china double wash-basins or the pretty tiles in the hall. Sunlight pours through the many windows, adding to the polished, genteel charm. Tapestries, oriental rugs on wooden floors, antiques and ornate mirrors, all contribute to the château's delightful Edwardian flavour.

During the First World War, the château was a military convalescence home. Among the soldiers who stayed there was Mme Bonand's nephew, Alan Seeger, who had been born in the United States but joined the Foreign Legion at the outbreak of the war. While staying at Château du Clair de Lune he wrote his celebrated poem, *J'ai un rendez-vous avec la mort*. Shortly afterwards, he returned to the front and on 2 July 1916 he was killed at the Somme. On 22 July 1972, the municipality of Biarritz paid tribute to the poet's love of France and of liberty by giving his name to the small road that leads to the château.

---

123 CHATEAU D'ILBARRITZ H

★

64210 Bidart, Pyrénées-Atlantiques.
Tel: 59 23 00 27
Propr: Société d'Exploitation Hôtelière Paris Côte Basque
Director: M. Massiaux
Open: 1 Mar - 30 Nov

Twin with bath	6 B-C
Double with bath	5 B-C
Suite	1 D
Total rooms:	12

No lift. All rooms on ground-floor.

Restaurant: Open daily - 1 June - 15 Sept
Chef: Mme Luraschi-Poulain
Lunch: 1230 - 1400
Dinner: 1930 - 2230
Prix fixe: Menus at A & B
A la carte available
Demi-pension (3 days+) B
Specialities:*Magret de canard aux myrtilles; Gratin de turbot au champagne.*

Groups: max. 20

Credit cards:
American Express
Diners Club
Visa
English & Spanish spoken

By the sea
Golf course 1km
Horse riding 1km

Châteaux et Demeures de Tradition

Bidart is just to the south of Biarritz and 1.5km from Autoroute 63. It is impossible to miss the château. On a promontory by the sea, it dominates the village. **Airport:** *Biarritz (6km)* **Station:** *Biarritz (6km)*

If we hadn't come across this château, we might never have heard of Baron Albert de l'Espée. That would have been a great loss - for he was, without doubt, one of the world's great eccentrics. It was towards the end of the last century that the Baron, who was then one of the world's richest men, decided to build on a spur overlooking the sea this extraordinary château, incorporating all his bizarre ideas and inventions. Four hundred workmen managed to complete everything in two years - the château was connected by covered walks to strange pavilions and the shore; there were underground caverns for the kitchens and the storage of his own special food. In summer the air was kept fresh by huge blocks of ice placed in marble troughs outside each window; in winter the rooms were kept warm by a central-heating system supplemented by bright lights fitted into the same marble troughs outside the windows. Admitting no visitors and having exiled his wife to the family estate, the Duke lived alone in the house with his two hundred servants and his mistress, the singer Biana Duhamel, for whom he'd built a villa in the grounds. When she departed, the Baron - by way of consolation - installed in the three-storey château the third largest pipe organ ever built in France. Constantly believing that contact with the world outside would be bad for his health, he tried to devise a system to ensure that the sea-water in which he bathed had been previously purified. Then, it is said, the Baron read a statement by a Parisian doctor that sea-air was bad for the health. On a whim, he left the château one day in 1912, never to return.

Over the years, the château was stripped and pillaged and became a ruin and an eyesore. It was bought in 1958 by M. Massiaux to convert into a small hotel. It has not been restored to its original grandeur - but some of the original spirit still survives. The organ room has been converted into a chapel where on Sundays a traditional Latin mass is said by the priests of Monsignor Lefebvre.

124 CHATEAU DE CASTELPERS H

★

Castelpers, 12170 Réquista, Aveyron.
Tel: 65 69 22 61
Propr: Mme Tapie de Celeyran
Open: 1 Apr - 30 Sep

Twin with showers	3 A-B
Twin with bath	1 B
Double with showers	2 A-B
Double with bath	2 B
Total rooms:	8

No lift. 2 ground-floor rooms.

Restaurant: Closed Tue, except for residents
Dinner: 1930 - 2030
Prix fixe: 3 menus at A
A la carte available
Demi-pension (3 days+) A-B
Specialities: *Confit de canard aux cèpes; Canette à l'ananas.*

Seminars: max. 25
Groups: max. 15
Credit cards:
Visa
Eurocard
Spanish spoken

Fishing
Swimming 1km
Tennis court 2km
Horse riding 14km

43km south-west of Rodez. From there, take the N88 to Naucelle. Turn left on the D10 to Castelpers. **Airport:** *Rodez (45km)* **Station:** *Naucelle (10km)*

Castelpers and its château are set amidst spectacular scenery in the Viaur Valley. The collection of buildings that make up the stone-walled château show that it has been considerably extended over the centuries - one part with a simple, rustic appearance is next to another far grander section with large arched windows. The château has been in the possession of the same family since 1650 and is now run as a simple, comfortable and inexpensive hotel. Some antique furniture gives character to the dining room and lounge. The bedrooms vary, but are all comfortable. A terrace overlooks the wooded grounds which stretch down to a small trout stream.

125 HOSTELLERIE DU LEVEZOU H

⛨ ★★
12410 Salles-Curan, Aveyron.
Tel: 65 46 34 16
Propr: M. David Bouviala
Open: 1 Apr - 15 Oct

Twin with shower	8 A
Twin with bath	9 B
Double with shower	6 A
Total rooms:	23

No lift

Restaurant: Closed Sun eve & Mon in low season
Chef: M. Hervé Michel
Lunch: 1230 - 1400
Dinner: 1930 - 2100
Prix fixe: Menus at A & B
A la carte available
Demi-pension (4 days+) A-B
Specialities: *Feuilleté de ris d'agneau sautés aux morilles à la crème, Râble de lapereau flambé au capucin et son saupiquet.*

Seminars: max. 40
Groups: max. 40
Credit cards:
American Express
Diners Club
Eurocard
Visa
English & Spanish spoken

Tennis court 500m
Pareloup Lake 1km

Châteaux Hôtels Indép.

37km north-east of Millau. From there, take the D911 towards Rodez. After 10km, turn right on the D30. At Bouloc, turn right on to the D993 to Salles-Curan. **Airport:** *Rodez (44km)* **Station:** *Rodez (37km)*

This fourteenth-century château was once the summer residence of the Bishop of Rodez. The ancient stone building, with its single round tower, has been satisfactorily converted into a modern hotel. But the greatest joy in discovering Levézou is the food. There is a vast range of traditional French cuisine and regional dishes to choose from and all are prepared with flair and sparkle. The recently awarded Michelin rosette is well deserved and the reasonable prices make each meal a bargain. There is a pleasant arched dining room, but on summer evenings it is far better to eat out in the vine-shaded courtyard. Strongly recommended!

CARAMAN MIDI-PYRENEES - Haute-Garonne

126 CHATEAU DU CROZILLAT PG

♥♥♥ ★★ ♆
31460 Caraman, Haute-Garonne.
Tel: 61 83 10 09
Propr: M. Bernard Guerin
Open: 15 Mar - 15 Dec

Twin with shower	2 B
Twin with bath	2 B
Suite (max. 4)	1 C
(inc. breakfast)	
Total rooms:	5

No lift. 1 ground-floor room.

Table d'hôte (res. only)
Dinner: 2000
Cuisin maison, specialités du pays.

Seminars: max. 12
Groups: max. 12

No credit cards
English & German spoken

Swimming pool
Horse riding
Golf practice

Les Etapes Francois Coeur
Gîtes de France

32km east of Toulouse. 20km north of the Villefranche-de-Lauragais exit on Autoroute 61, from where take the D25 to Caraman. Turn right on to the D1 and the long drive to the château is a further 2km on the right. **Airport:** *Toulouse (37km)* **Station:** *Revel (21km) or Toulouse*

At the end of a long drive, dappled with the shade of ancient plane trees, stands this beautiful old château. Surrounded by fragrant flower-beds, mature trees, clipped bushes and carefully tended lawns, it is a dignified and tranquil place with great charm.

The various parts of the château were built between the thirteenth and sixteenth centuries for the de Villeneuve family, who lived there for over five hundred years. Towards the end of the sixteenth century, during the Wars of Religion, the château and the village of Caraman were set on fire and partially destroyed. The rebuilding that took place afterwards created the present château with its single round tower, a castellated keep and one of its two wings with a tiled-roof so gradually sloped that it's almost flat. On the opposite side of the courtyard to the main building is an immaculate stable-block, which houses the owner's horses and foals.

Bernard Guerin's grand-father bought the château in 1923 and so it has been in his family for some time. His home is clearly Bernard Guerin's great passion. For many years he was a Parisian auctioneer and an avid collector of fine antiques.

With these and original pieces belonging to his family and previous owners, he has furnished the château. A man with great sensitivity and flair, he has created a place of great beauty that is obviously a family home and not a museum or a collection of showrooms. Delightful surprises are encountered around every corner - an ancient rocking-horse, a gilded madonna, Javanese shadow-puppets. The decorations are designed to provide a perfect background. Many of the floors are polished wood with Persian rugs. The sitting-room has comfortable modern furniture as well as gorgeous antiques. The dining room is magnificent. At either end of the house is a flight of stone steps that leads to the bedrooms, all of which are different, but equally attractive, delightfully furnished and extremely comfortable. Most have an extra bed that can be used by children.

The careful, stylish restoration work on the château still continues. In 1987, an ancient arched cellar was excavated and the wonderful stone-work cleaned. Further projects will no doubt follow. Yet there is about Crozillat none of the antiseptic air found in châteaux that have been expensively converted into luxury hotels. This is a family home to which guests are enthusiastically invited. Bernard Guerin is a charming, relaxed and intelligent man who says that, in opening his home to others, he wishes to continue the tradition, maintained over the centuries, of offering at Crozillat a warm welcome, openness and a spirit of freedom.

LARRA - Grenade MIDI-PYRENEES - Haute-Garonne

127 CHATEAU DE LARRA PG

♥♥ ★
Larra, 31330 Grenade, Haute-Garonne.
Tel: 61 82 62 51
Propr: Baronne de Carrière
Open: All year

No lift. 3 ground-floor rooms.

Double with shower 2 B
Double with bath 2 B
(inc. breakfast)
Total rooms: 4
Each has extra room available
Table d'hôte (res. only) A
Dinner: 20.00
Specialities: *Magret grillé; Armagnac.*

No credit cards
English spoken

Horse-riding 1km
Tennis court 1 km

Gîtes de France
Les Etapes Francois Coeur

31km north-west of Toulouse. From there, take the D1 past the airport. After Montaigut-sur-Save and crossing the river, turn right onto the D87. After 4km, turn left to Larra. At a junction in the village, turn left and the drive to the château is on the right. **Airport:** *Toulouse (27km)* **Station:** *Toulouse (31km)*

Château de Larra looks most bizarre. It is a beautiful, finely-proportioned eighteenth-century mansion on top of which is perched, in the most ungainly fashion, a monstrous shanty-pagoda. This absurd addition was constructed as a book-filled retreat by the present owner's eccentric uncle. He sought to avoid the company of everyone, including his wife. Perhaps in an effort to bring visitors' eyes back to ground-level, Baronne de Carrière has arranged a beautiful display of orange and lemon trees around the otherwise rather bleak front courtyard.

The interior of the château is astonishing. In the massive and extremely grand entrance hall, vast urns of orchids and other exotic plants stand on the marble-tiled floor. The lofty ceiling is heavily beamed and the white walls are decorated with ornate rococo embellishments picked out in green. At the far end, a wide flight of stairs sweeps up to the floor above. Around the stair-case, almost every inch of wall space is covered with oil paintings of various sizes, ornate mirrors, engravings and tiny water colours.

Off this fantastic hall are three of the bedrooms. Ours was an odd mixture of the old and the new. The carpet was a brown-patterned nylon, the walls were purple and the flowers plastic. The new bath was midget-size and the toilet was equipped with the open-jaws system of flushing. It is, however, the least attractive room and the others are much more pleasant.

Upstairs, the salon on the landing is a wonderful room - bright, spacious and elegant, with a romantic air of faded grandeur. The dining room is unremarkable, but the food is delicious.

Beside the château is what once must have been a perfect formal garden. Totally walled, it is delightful, although, like the house, it has clearly seen more prosperous times. But still the fragrance from the many rose bushes fills the air and peacocks strut across the lawns. Their eerie cries echo through the calm evening air and are part of the unusual experience of a stay at the Château de Larra.

128 CHATEAU DE JOTTES PG

Lherm, 31600 Le Muret, Haute-Garonne.
Tel: 61 56 03 60
Propr: M. Claude & Mme Nicole Clairac
Open: Easter - 31 Oct

Twin with shower	1 A
Twin with bath	2 A
Double with bath	2 A
Suite (in annexe)	1 C
Total rooms:	6

Table d'hôte (res. only) B
Chef: Mme Nicole Clairac
Dinner: 20.00
Demi pension (7 days+) A

No lift

Groups: max. 14
Receptions: max. 350
No credit cards
English spoken

Horse riding 1km

Gîtes de France

30km south-west of Toulouse. From there, take the N117. Take the second exit for Muret and turn right on the D3 towards Rieumes. At Labastidette, turn left on the D23 to Lherm, where take the D43 towards Rieumes. The château is 1km on the left. **Airport:** *Toulouse (32km)* **Station:** *Muret (9km)*

This is not a château for the faint-hearted. The drive passes a car-breaker's yard and enters under an archway into what appears to be the timeless tranquillity of a courtyard surrounded by ancient buildings. This illusion is immediately shattered as four enormous Alsatians, barking savagely, imprison cautious visitors in their car, until they are rescued by either the owners or one of their family.

M. and Mme Clairac bought the château in 1979 when it was a roofless ruin, with plants growing inside. Although the restoration-work continues, the château is already an extremely popular spot in the locality for holding boisterous wedding ceremonies, when up to five hundred people carouse and dance the night away in the courtyard. The Clairacs also run a furniture business in the old stables.

Inside, the château is a huge, rather dark place, though a semi-circular ballroom added in the late eighteenth century is quite stunning, with gilt rococo decorations, a high ceiling and huge windows. Upstairs there are many long dark corridors, off which are the rather basic bedrooms and communal w.c.s. If you would like to sample a French country wedding celebration - and they are jolly occasions - try almost any Saturday night.

129 CHATEAU BELLEVUE H

19 Rue Joseph Cappin,
32150 Cazaubon, Gers.
Tel: 62 09 51 95
Telex: 521 429 F
Propr: M. Michele Consolaro
Open: 1 Mar - 31 Dec

Twin with shower	1 A
Twin with bath	12 B
Double with bath	12 B
Total rooms:	25

Lift

Restaurant: Open daily
Chef: M. Bruno Roussel
Lunch: 1230 - 1400
Dinner: 1930 - 2100
Prix fixe: Menus at A & B
A la carte available
Demi-pension (3 days+) B
Specialities: *Soupe de palombes* (woodpigeon) *au celeri boule; Cassolette d'escargots au foie gras et à l'ail; Escalopes de foie gras de canard aux pointes d'asperges.*

Seminars: max. 40
Groups: max. 40
Credit cards:
American Express
Diners Club
Visa
English, German, Spanish & Italian spoken

Swimming pool
Tennis court 1km
Lake 1km
Golf course 30km

La Castellerie

40km east of Mont-de-Marsan. From there, take the D952. After 10km, fork right on to the D933. At Saint-Justin, turn right on the D626 to Cazaubon. **Airport:** *Agen (72km)* **Station:** *Mont-de-Marsan (40km)*

In the centre of the Armagnac region, this late eighteenth century château has a small flower garden and park. Bought by the present owner's family in 1956, it was converted into an hotel in 1970. Neither the exterior nor the interior of the building has any specific style, but everywhere is pleasant and comfortable. Paintings are exhibited on the walls. The rooms vary in size and in their decoration - some have beds with canopies, and others, on the upper floor, have beamed ceilings. As in many straightforward rural hotels such as this, it is the food that is most important - and it is very good, including a number of traditional Gascony dishes.

GIMONT-EN-GASCOGNE MIDI-PYRENEES - Gers

130 CHATEAU DE LARROQUE H

★★

32200 Gimont, Gers.
Tel: 62 67 77 44
Telex: 531 135 F
Propr: M. Célestin Fagedet
Open: 1 Mar - 31 Dec

Double with bath	15 B-D
Suite	1 G
Total rooms:	16

No lift

Restaurant: Open daily
Chef: M. André Fagedet
Lunch: 1200 - 1430
Dinner: 1930 - 2130
Prix fixe: Menus at A & B
A la carte available
Demi-pension (3 days+) C
Specialities: *Pigeon à l'ail confit; Jarret de porc aux poires; Emincés de pintade à la crème de citron.*

Seminars: max. 50
Groups: max. 30
Receptions: max. 150
Credit cards:
American Express
Diners Club
Visa
English spoken

Tennis court
Swimming pool 2km

Relais & Châteaux

53km west of Toulouse. From there, take the N124. The château is on the left, just before entering Gimont. **Airport:** *Toulouse (50km)* **Station:** *Gimont (1km)*

Perhaps we visited this château at a bad time, but it appeared to us to have a rather tense atmosphere. It was a pity for otherwise this hotel has a lot to offer. The food is good, the grounds are splendid and the interior decorations are mostly plain and pleasing colours. A bold racing-green carpet covers the stairs and landings. The bedrooms are attractive, particularly a small one on the second floor that has been decorated in a delicate apricot colour. Downstairs, the lounge is cool and restful, with a high beamed ceiling, an enormous fireplace, a polished stone floor, and modern furniture. There are several, different-sized dining rooms. The smallest has violet-coloured walls, beige and brown carpet and blue table-cloths covered with white lace. The largest one has red and beige wallpaper, red table-cloths with a beige-lace covering, and a green carpet. We welcome reports!

LACAVE - Souillac MIDI-PYRENEES - Lot

131 CHATEAU DE LA TREYNE PG

♛♛♛ ★★★ ▼
Lacave, 46200 Souillac, Lot.
Tel: 65 32 66 66
Telex: 531 427 F
Propr: Mme Michèle Gombert- Devals
Open: Easter - 3 Jan

Double with bath	10 C-D
Suites	2 E
Total rooms:	12

No lift

Restaurant (guests only): Open every day
Prix fixe: 1 menu at B
A la carte available
Demi-pension C-D
Specialities: *Truffe sous la cendre dans son feuilleté; Escalopes de saumon au coulis de persil et leurs pleurottes* (mushrooms) *craquantes; Marquise au chocolat et sa sauce pistache; Soufflé chaud aux framboises.*

Groups: max. 20
Credit cards:
American Express
Diners Club
Visa
English spoken

Swimming pool
Tennis court
Billiards
Sauna
Ballooning
Beside Dordogne
Châteaux Accueil
Châteaux Hôtels Indép.
Les Etapes Francois Coeur
Indepen. Leading Association

46km south of Brive-la-Gaillarde. From there, take the N20 to Souillac. Pass through the village and, just before the bridge over the Dordogne, turn left on to the narrow D43 which runs along side the river. The château will shortly be seen on a cliff on the opposite side. The D43 eventually crosses the Dordogne and the entrance to the château is just afterwards on the right. **Airport:** *Brive (49km)* **Station:** *Souillac (8km)*

Perched high on a rocky bluff beside a graceful meander in the Dordogne, this gleaming-white château, with its slate-topped roofs and towers, is stunning. As we drove over the narrow bridge towards it and then up the long drive, shaded by ancient trees, we feared that it would be impossible for the reality to live up to the first glorious impression. To make matters worse, we were committing the cardinal sin of arriving at lunch-time on a Sunday. We parked the car and crunched across the shingled forecourt to find that the heavy, studded oak door was just being closed. But as soon as we were seen it was flung open again and we were given the warmest of welcomes. At Château de la Treyne it is obvious that the guests come first. During our stay, we were to discover that it is in many other ways an exceptional place. The setting, the warmth and friendliness of the proprietor and her staff, the general atmosphere and the interior are as impressive as the first sight of the exterior.

A château was first built on the site in the fourteenth century but, like so many other fortified properties in the region, it was burned down during the Wars of Religion. Château de la Treyne was rebuilt in the early part of the seventeenth century.

When the château opened as an hotel in the mid-1980s, Mme Gombert-Devals had transformed the interior. The vast sitting-room is impressive, with its high panelled ceiling and tiled marble floor. Around the door is an ornate, painted wooden surround and the room is lit by sparkling chandeliers. With high-backed chairs grouped around small tables and a grand-piano in one corner, it is the ideal place for the musical soirées held there or for a convivial drink.

The bedrooms are delightful. Those off the second floor have been recently refurbished with harmonising colour-schemes, luxurious bedding and marbled bathrooms. On the floor below, the bedrooms are more sombre but extremely impressive, including one where the walls are hung with padded silk. There are high beamed ceilings, tall mirrors and four-poster beds. The bathrooms too are splendid - the one in the Empire Room having a huge old bath and a giant double wash-basin.

Then there is the swimming pool, the sauna, the excellent restaurant, and the magnificent grounds, in which stands a Romanesque chapel. But our favourite spot is the terrace, where on warm summer evenings guests dine, while below the Dordogne flows on to the sea.

LOUBRESSAC - Bretenoux MIDI-PYRENEES - Lot

132 CHATEAU DE GAMOT PG

Loubressac, 46130
Bretenoux, Lot.
Tel: 65 38 52 05, 65 38 58 50
Propr: Mme Annie Bellières
Open: July & August

No lift

Double with bath 2 A
Double - shared w.c. 3 A
(inc. breakfast)
Total rooms: 5
(4 rooms have a small room attached for children)

No restaurant

No credit cards
English spoken

Swimming pool
By the Dordogne

Gîtes de France

A 34km drive through magnificent scenery north-east of Rocamadour. From there, take the D673 towards Montal. After 17km, turn left on the tiny D38. At Montal turn left on to the D30. Just after reaching the Dordogne, the château is on the left.

From the outside, Gamot is not a particularly attractive château. With a single tower, the small stone building was erected on the site of an ancient chapel. Inside is very different. The floors are beautiful, polished oak boards. All around there are old pieces of furniture that have been in the family for generations. Wide stairs lead to an enormous landing. The bedrooms are simple, but appealing, and all have been recently redecorated. Breakfast is served in the large airy kitchen around a long refectory table. The small garden is overgrown, and the surrounding land is cultivated. The château is owned by a Parisian doctor, who returns during the summer. That is why it is open only in July and August.

133 CHATEAU DE ROUMEGOUSE H

★★★
Rignac-2C- 46500 Gramat, Lot.
Tel: 65 33 63 81
Telex: 532 592 F
Propr: M. Jean-Louis & Mme Luce Lainé
Open: 1 Apr - 1 Nov

Twin with bath	6 B-D
Double with bath	6 B-D
Suites (max. 4)	3 D
Total rooms:	15

No lift. 2 rooms and 1 suite on ground floor

Restaurant: Closed Tue, except in July & August
Chef: M. Yarmick Bruneau
Lunch: 1230 - 1345
Dinner: 1930 - 2100
Prix fixe: Menus at A & B
A la carte available
Demi-pension C-D
Specialities: *Foie gras; Truffes; Confit canard.*

Groups: max. 20
Receptions: max. 50
Credit cards:
American Express
Diners Club
Eurocard
Visa
English & Spanish spoken

Swimming pool
Tennis courts 3km
Horse riding 3km

Relais & Châteaux

54km south of Brive-la-Gaillarde. From there, take the N20. Ater 20km, at Cressensac, fork left on to the N140. The road to the château is on the left, 1km after the village of Blanat. **Airport:** *Brive (60km)* **Station:** *Gramat (3km)*

A narrow lane winds uphill past drystone walls, tiny cottages and a farmyard before eventually reaching the imposing Château de Roumégouse. Built in medieval times, it was totally renovated at the end of the nineteenth century. The interior was refurbished in a surpisingly pleasant neo-Gothic style. In 1965, the château was purchased by Mme Lainé's parents and after ten months' extremely hard work was converted into an excellent, stylish hotel. Since it was opened, Roumégouse has been visited by many famous guests, including General de Gaulle, President Pompidou and Raymond Queneau.

M. and Mme Lainé are now the proprietors of the hotel. Jean-Louis Lainé is an amusing and entertaining host with a wry sense of humour. He bears an uncanny resemblance to James Cagney in his heyday, which explains the constant nagging feeling that you've met him somewhere before.

The rooms are spacious and most pleasing. The salon is a striking room -

carpeted and curtained in a bright rose-colour, with a royal blue ceiling and violet velvet covering the chairs. Standing on a dark blue Persian rug in the centre of the room is an antique table and on it a glorious arrangement of fresh flowers. Most of the bedrooms are more subdued, although one contains an extravagant, ornately carved bed, complete with canopy, in the Gothic style of the mid-sixteenth century. The others, decorated in rose or pink or mauve, are prettily furnished with antique chests, small tables and ornate mirrors. All are large and fully carpeted.

The meals, like the château, are delightful, with a pleasing sense of richness and luxury. M. and Mme Lainé clearly have a eye for detail, both in the dining room and the rest of the hotel. So, for example, excellent touring itineraries are given to guests. Even the cleaners are arrayed in pretty pink track-suits!

MERCUES - Cahors MIDI-PYRENEES - Lot

134 CHATEAU DE MERCUES H

♛♛♛ ★★★
Mercuès, 46090 Cahors, Lot.
Tel: 65 20 00 01
Telex: 521 307 F
Propr: M. Georges Vigouroux
Direc: M. Yves & Mme Brigitte Buchin
Open: 1 Mar - 31 Oct

Twin with bath	5	C-E
Double with bath	11	C-E
Suites (max. 5)	7	E-H
Total rooms:	23	

Lift. 3 ground-floor rooms & facilities for handicapped.

Restaurant: Open daily
Chef: M. Hervé Guerin
Lunch: 1230 - 1400
Dinner: 1930 - 2130
Prix fixe: Menus at A & B
A la carte available
Demi-pension C-F
Specialities: *Foie gras frais de canard; Daube* (stew) *de canard aux Comtes de Cahors; Salade de pommes de terre aux truffes; Escalope de foie gras au château de Haute-Serre.*

Seminars: max. 35
Groups: max. 20
Credit cards:
American Express
Diners Club
Eurocard
Visa
English & German spoken

Swimming pool
Tennis courts
Helipad
Horse riding 2km

Relais & Châteaux

6km north-west of Cahors. From there, take the D911 towards Villeneuve-sur-Lot. In Mercuès, turn right and the road winds up to the château.
Airport: *Toulouse (102km)* **Station:** *Cahors (6km)*

Overlooking the Lot Valley, Château de Mercuès stands on a hill where the Romans built a temple. The castle was built in the thirteenth century as a protection for the town of Cahors and as a residence for its bishop who, being also a count, wielded absolute sovereignty over the area. As with all such ancient castles, its history is a complex story of occupations, destruction, rebuilding, pillaging and abandonment. But for most of its history, it was the palace of successive bishops of Cahors. One of these, in 1861, ordered its extension and modernisation. The present external appearance of the château dates from that period.

In 1904, at the time of the separation of the church and state, the Bishop of Cahors abandoned the residence and it was sold to Professor Jean-Louis Faure, a surgeon. When he died in 1944, his home was turned into a château-hotel by his daughters. But it was not until the property was purchased in 1966 by Georges Hereil, the president of Simca, that Mercuès was converted, after a vast amount of work, into the luxurious establishment that soon won international acclaim. Then, in 1980, Georges Hereil died, and the château was locked up and left abandoned.

On 1 September 1983, it was acquired by Georges Vigouroux, whose family owned extensive vineyards in the area. He undertook the total restoration of the exterior and the refurbishment of the interior. Yves and Brigitte Buchin were appointed as directors. When the hotel opened the following summer, it was feared by many that it would not approach its previous high standards. But the pessimists were confounded - the hotel had been given a new, luxurious lease of life. In 1987, it was accepted as a Relais & Châteaux hotel.

The bedrooms differ in size and in decorations - but all are elegantly furnished and comfortable, with delightful views of the surrounding countryside. The most astonishing room is in one of the suites in a tower. At a push of a button the wooden joists of the turret are revealed - apparently in this room one of the bishops of Cahors who was an astronomer had tracked the course of the planets on the polished floorboards! The cuisine of the chef, Hervé Guerin, has won high praise for its varied and interesting dishes. There is a fine wine list, which naturally features the splendid full-bodied Cahors reds produced by Georges Vigouroux, including the delightful Château de Mercuès, appellation Cahors.

SAINT-PIERRE-LA-FEUILLE MIDI-PYRENEES - Lot

135 CHATEAU DE ROUSSILLON PG

46000 Saint-Pierre-La-Feuille, Lot.
Tel: 65 36 87 05
Propr: M. Marcelle Hourriez
Open: All year

No lift. Ground-floor room.

Double with bath 1 B (inc. breakfast)
Apartments: 1

Table d'hôte (res. only) A

Seminars: max. 100
Receptions: max. 100
No credit cards
English spoken

Swimming pool 10km
Tennis courts 10km

Gîtes de France

10km north of Cahors. From there, take the N20. At Saint-Pierre-La-Feuille, turn right to the château. **Airport:** *Cahors (26km)* **Station:** *Cahors (10km)*

Standing on a rocky promontory, this half-ruined medieval castle dominates the whole of the region. It was built between the thirteenth and fifteenth centuries on the site of an older fortress. Six towers originally stood in the massive outer walls. Inside was a courtyard leading to a keep. This controlled the entrance to the three main buildings, one of which had its own tower containing a staircase. Because the castle overlooked the main road to the north from Cahors, Roussillon played an important part in the bitter and protracted wars of the middle ages. But when these ended, the castle ceased to be occupied - its owners, no longer needing its protection, preferred to live in more comfortable and elegant surroundings. The courtyard of Roussillon became a farmyard and chickens roosted in the dilapidated buildings. During the French Revolution, the castle, seen as a symbol of feudalism, was attacked by the mob. Some of its stones were taken to build houses in the area - a process that continued throughout the nineteenth century. In 1958, Marcelle Hourriez bought the ruined castle and converted what remained of the old buildings into simple rooms for receptions and seminars. Limited accommodation is also available.

136 CHATEAU DE GARREVAQUES

PG

🛡🛡★★
Garrevaques, 81700 Puylaurens, Tarn.
Tel: 63 75 04 54, 61 52 01 47
Telex: 530 955 F
Propr: Mme Barande & Mme Marie-Christine Combes
Open: All year (reservation in winter)

No lift

Twin with bath	4	C
Double with shower	1	C
Double with bath	3	C
Suites (max. 5) (inc. breakfast)	2	D
Total rooms:	10	
Apartments:	1	

Table d'hôte (res. only) A
Chef: Mme Solange
Demi-pension (3 days+) B
Specialities: *Suprême de canard au sang sauce salmis; Faisandeau flambé au cognac.*

Seminars: max. 30
Groups: max. 15
Receptions: max. 120
Credit cards: Visa
English & Spanish spoken

Swimming pool
Tennis court
Horse riding 10km
Golf course 25km

Château Accueil

25km north of Autoroute A61 and Castelnaudary. From there, take the D624. After 15km, at the junction with the D622, turn right to Revel. Pass through the town on the D622 and after 2km turn left on the D24 to Garrevaques. The château is just beyond the village on the right.
Airport: *Toulouse (56km)* **Station:** *Castelnaudary (25km)*

Mme Marie-Christine Combes is an energetic and extremely busy woman. She not only helps her mother run Château Garrevaques, but she is a vice-president of Château Accueil. Not surprisingly, therefore, Garrevaques is one of the best known privately-owned châteaux accepting paying guests.

Although a château was built on the site in 1470 by ancestors of the present owners, it was destroyed during the French Revolution. The château that exists today was built in the early part of the nineteenth century. It is a solid edifice somewhat lacking in baronial presence with its plain red brick and stucco finish.

However, there is nothing plain about the welcome of Mme Barande and her two daughters. They are enthusiastic and energetic hostesses who provide guests with much help, including prepared touring itineraries.

Much of the interior is interesting, especially the salon at the entrance. On its walls is early nineteenth-century, hand-painted paper, depicting grey-and-white classical scenes - a rare example of a forerunner of modern wallpaper. There is also an attractive sitting room with gilt-framed mirrors, chandeliers, delicate furniture and - like most of the rooms - a parquet floor. The dining room is large and sombre, which may be a relief when the sun is blazing. The bedrooms are pleasant enough and in most rooms throughout the château there are antique pieces of furniture.

Garrevaques provides guests with an opportunity to share the daily life of an ancient French family.

137 CHATEAU DE MONTLEDIER H

★

Route d'Anglès, 81660 Pont-de-l'Arn (Mazamet), Tarn.
Tel: 63 61 20 54
Telex: 531 833 chamco
Propr: M. & Mme Thiercelin
Open: 1 Feb - 31 Dec
Closed: January

Double with bath 9 B-C
No lift.

Restaurant: Closed Sunday dinner & Mondays (except July, Sept & August)
Lunch: 1230 - 1400
Dinner: 1945 - 2130
Prix fixe: Menus at A & B
A la carte available

Credit cards:
American Express
Diners Club
Visa
Eurocard
English spoken

Inter. Leading Association

4.5km east of Mazamet. From there, take the N112. After 1km, turn left on the D54 which winds up the mountain side. The drive to the château is a further 3km on the right. **Airport:** *Carcassonne (52km)* **Station:** *Mazamet (5km)*

The most memorable thing about this château is the spectacular journey necessary to reach it. As we drove further and further up the mountain, we watched in amazement as a swirling mist slowly filled the beautiful valley below and gusted hazardously across the road ahead. Not knowing quite where we were going to end up, we were very relieved to discover the narrow drive that led to Château de Montledier.

Originally built in the thirteenth century, the stone-walled château was later converted into a country house. By the middle of this century, it was in ruins. Christine and Francis Sidobre enthusiastically restored it and, in 1988, the small hotel they had established was acquired by the present owners, M. and Mme Thiercelin. They have redecorated some of the bedrooms, but there are still some that sport the most vivid of colours — golds and scarlets in bold-patterned cloth on bedspreads, curtains, canopies and even headboards. In contrast, the downstairs rooms, including the dining-room, have a much less striking, almost rustic appearance, with simple furniture, rough-cast walls and stone-flagged floors.

Although a quiet, out-of-the-way spot, Château de Montleidier provides an ideal base for touring the spectacular Tarn countryside.

138 CHATEAU SAINT-ROCH PG

♥♥ ★
Le Pin, 82340 Auvillar, Tarn-et-Garonne.
Tel: 63 95 95 22
Fax: 56 61 18 78
Telex: 550 503F
Propr: M. André Sagne
Open: 1 Mar - 31 Dec

Double	7 B-D
Suite	1 D
Total rooms:	8

No lift

Table d'hôte on reservation

Seminars: max. 25
English spoken

Tennis court
Swimming pool 10km
Horse riding 10 km
Golf course 12km

Châteaux Hôtels Indép.
Les Etapes Francois Coeur

Close to Autoroute 62 (exit 8) and 14km south-east of Valence. From there, take the D953 over the rivers, and at Mondou turn left on the D12 through Auvillar. After 8km, turn right to Le Pin. As you reach the village, the entrance to the château is on the right. **Airport:** *Agen (38km)* **Station:** *Valence (14km)*

This vast, early nineteenth-century château is extraordinary. Steeply roofed and turreted outside, it has an interior that strongly resembles a prosperous Victorian town hall. Everything is on a gigantic scale and is most ornate. There is a great deal of oak panelling. The wooden ceilings are carved and painted with red and gold motifs. The floor-tiles have intricate designs in blue, green and yellow. In the salon is a colossal white fire-surround - on either side, a bare-breasted caryatid and a bearded atlantes are bowed beneath the weight of the huge overmantle. The ornate wallpaper is navy, red, gold and blue. All the furniture is of the period - heavy and cumbersome. Depending on your taste, the whole neo-Gothic building may be a marvel or a monstrosity. Either way, it's certainly worth a visit.

Since M. Sagne took over the château in 1988, a considerable amount of money has been spent on renovating and refurbishing the bathrooms and bedrooms, all of which are now first-class.

Index of Chateaux

ARBIEU - Bazas 111
ARTANNES - Artannes-sur-Indre 59
ARTIGNY - Montbazon 71
AUBIGNY - Marseilles-les-Aubigny 48
AUDRIEU - Audrieu 1
AULNAYE - Nogent-le-Rotrou 54
AYRES - Meyrueis 156

BASME - Couddes 81
BEAULIEU - Joué-lès-Tours 64
BEAULIEU - Savigné-sur-Lathan 79
BEAUVOIS - Luynes 69
BELLEVUE - Cazaubon 129
BERGERON - Soustons 116
BEUVRIERE - Grez-Neuville 41
BEUVRIERE - Saint-Hilaire-de-Court 50
BLOSSES - Saint-Ouen-la-Rouerie 31
BRECOURT - Douains 11
BRINDOS - Anglet 121
BRIOTTIERES — Champigne 38
BUROS - Gabarret 115

CAMIAC ET SAINT-DENIS - Camiac et Saint-Denis 112
CASTEL FERRON - Tonneins 120
CASTEL MARIE-LOUISE - La Baule 36
CASTEL MORPHEE - Gacé 18
CASTEL NOVEL - Varetz 102
CASTELPERS - Réquista 124
CELLE-GUENAND - La Celle-Guenand 65
CHANTECAILLE - Mer 84
CHEMAN - Blaison 37
CHEMILLY - Langeais 66
CHICAMOUR - Sury-aux-Bois 92
CHISSAY - Chissay-en-Touraine 80
CINQ-MARS - Cinq-Mars-le-Pile 63
CLAIR DE LUNE - Biarritz 122
COATGUELEN - Pléhédel 23
COLLIERS - Muids-sur-Loire 84
COMMARQUE - Sauternes 114
COMANDERIE - Farges-Allichamps 46
COULAINE - Beaumont-en-Veron 61
CRAON - Craon 44
CROZILLAT - Caraman 126

DANZAY - Beaumont-en-Veron 62
DIANE - Ecrainville 20

EPANVILLIERS - Brux 97
ESCLIMONT - Saint-Symphorien-le-Château 55
ESTIVEAUX - Le Châtelet-en-Berry 47

FERRIERE - Châteaubriant 35
FLEURAC - Fleurac 92

GAMOT - Loubressac 132
GARREVAQUES - Garrevaques 136
GERFAUT - Azay-le-Rideau 58
GOVILLE - Le-Breuil-en-Bessin 4
GRIFFERAIE - Echemiré 40
GUE-PEAN - Menthou-sur-Cher 85

HAUTE BORDE - Rilly-sur-Loire 89
HAUTS-DE-LOIRE - Onzaine 87

ILBARRITZ - Bidart 123

JOTTES - Lherm 128

KERAMBLEIZ - Plomelin 25
KERAVEON - Erdeven 32
KERMEZEN - Pommerit-Jaudy 24
KERNUZ - Pont-l'Abbé 26

LA FRANCEULE - Janzé 28
LA HUBERDIERE - Nazelles 74
LA MULONNIERE - Saint-Antoine-du-Rocher 76
LA RICARDIERE - Tourville 13
LALANDE - Razac-sur-l'Isle 107
LANDEL - Bézancourt 19
LARCAY - Larcay 67
LARRA - Larra 127
LARROQUE - Gimont-en-Gascogne 130
LE CASTEL - Bayeux 2
LE SEIGLAL - Monclar d'Agenais 117
LEAUVILLE - Landujan 29
LEVEZOU - Salles-Curan 125
LIVRAIE - Celle-l'Evescault 98
LOCGUENOLE - Hennebont 33

MAILLEBOIS - Maillebois 53
MALROME - Saint-André-du-Bois 113
MARCAY - Marcay 70
MAVALEIX - Mavaleix 104
MENAUDIERE - Montrichard 86
MERCUES - Mercuès 134
MILLY - Razines 75
MOLAY - Le Molay-Littry 5

MONTFORT - Muelles 7
MONTGOGER - Saint-Epian 77
MONTLEDIER - Pont de l'Arn 137
MONTOUR - Beaumont-en-Veron 76
MONTPOUPON - Montpoupon 73
MONTREUIL - Montreuil-sur-Loir 43
MONVIEL - Monviel 118
MOTHE - Artannes-sur-Indre 60
MOTTE BEAUMANOIR - Pleugueneuc 30
MOUNET-SULLY - Bergerac 103
MUIDS - La Ferté-Saint-Aubin 90

NANTEUIL - Huisseau-sur-Cosson 83
NIEUIL - Nieuil 94

OLBREUSE - Usseau 96

PERIGNY - Périgny 99
PLESSIS - La Jaille-Yvon 42
PRAY - Amboise 57
PRE D'AUGE - Pré d'Auge 6
PUY ROBERT - Montignac 106

QUENGO - Irodouer 27
QUINEVILLE - Quinéville 17

RAINFREVILLE - Tocqueville-en-Caux 21
RAPEE - Bazincourt-sur-Epte 10
RAULY-SAULIEUT -Monbazillac 104
REGAGNAC - Monterraud 105
REAUX - Le Port-Boulet 68
RIBAUTE - Ribaute-les-Tavernes 148
RIFFETS - Bretteville-sur-Laize 3
ROCHE-PICHEMER - Saint-Ouen-des-Vallons 45
ROCHECOTTE - Saint-Patrice 78
ROCHEUX - Fréteval 82
ROCHEVILAINE - Ponte de Pen-Lan 34
ROQUE - Hebecrevon 15
ROGNAC - Rognac 108
ROLLAND - Barsac 110
ROSAY - Rosay-sur-Lieure 12
ROUMEGOUSE - Rignac 133
ROUSSAINVILLE - Illiers-Combray 52
ROUSSILLON - Saint-Pierre-La-Feuille 135

SAINT-BONNET - Sérigny 100
SAINT-MARCEL - Agen 118
SAINT-PHILIP - Saint-Nicolas de la Balerme 119
SAINT-ROCH - Le Pin 138
SAINTE CATHERINE - Montbron 93

SALLE - Montpinchon 16
SALLES - Saint-Fort-sur-Gironde 95

TEILDRAS - Cheffes-sur-Sarthe 39
TERNAY - Ternay 101
TERTRES - Onzain 88
THAUMIERS - Thaumiers 51
TORTINIERE - Montbazon 72
TREYNE - Lacave 131

VAL D'ARGUENON - Notre Dame du Guildo 22
VALLEE BLEUE - Saint-Chartier 56
VAULAVILLE - Tour-en-Bessin 8
VAUMICEL - Vaumicel 9
VERRERIE - Oizon 49
VEYRIGNAC - Veyrignac 109
VIEUX CHATEAU - Bricquebec 14
VOUTE - Troo 90

Index of Places

AGEN, Château Saint-Marcel 118
AMBOISE, Château de Pray 57
ANGLET, Château de Brindos 121
ARTANNES-SUR-INDRE, Château d'Artannes 59
ARTANNES-SUR-INDRE, Château la Mothe 60
AUDRIEU, Château d'Audrieu 1
AZAY- LE-RIDEAU, Château du Gerfaut 58

BARSAC, Hostellerie du Château de Rolland 110
BAYEUX, Le Castel 2
BAZAS, Château d'Arbieu 111
BAZINCOURT-SUR-EPTE, Château de la Râpee 10
BEAUMONT-EN-VERON, Château de Coulaine 61
BEAUMONT-EN-VERON, Château de Danzay 62
BEAUMONT-EN-VERON, Manoir de Montour 75
BERGERAC, Château Mounet-Sully 103
BEZANCOURT, Château du Landel 19
BIARRITZ, Château du Clair de Lune 122
BIDART, Château d'Ilbarritz 123
BLAISON, Château de Cheman 37
BRETTEVILLE-SUR-LAIZE, Château des Riffets 3
BRICQUEBEC, Hôtel du Vieux Château 14
BRUX, Château d'Epanvilliers 97

CAMIAC ET SAINT-DENIS, Château Camiac et Saint-Denis 112
CARAMAN, Château du Crozillat 126
CAZAUBON, Château Bellevue 129
CELLE-L'EVESCAULT, Château de la Livraie 98
CHAMPIGNE, Château des Briottières 38
CHATEAUBRIANT, Hostellerie de la Ferrière 35
CHEFFES-SUR-SARTHE, Château de Teildras 39
CHISSAY-EN-TOURAINE, Château Hôtel-de-Chissay 80
CINQ-MARS-LA-PILE, Château de Cinq-Mars 63
COUDDES, Château de la Basme 81
CRAON, Château de Craon 44

DOUAINS, Château de Brécourt 11

ECHEMIRE, Château de la Grifferaie 40
EGRAINVILLE, Château de Diane 20
ERDEVEN, Château de Keraveon 32

FARGES-ALLICHAMPS, Château de la Commanderie 46
FLEURAC, Château de Fleurac 92
FRETEVAL, Château de Rocheux 82

GABARRET, Château de Buros 115
GACE, Castel Morphée 18
GARREVAQUES, Château de Garrevaques 136
GIMONT-EN-GASCOGNE, Château de Larroque 130
GREZ-NEUVILLE, Château de la Beuvrière 41

HEBECREVON, Château de la Roque 15
HENNEBONT, Château de Locguénolé 33
HUISSEAU-SUR-COSSON, Château de Nanteuil 83

ILLIERS-COMBRAY, Château de Roussainville 52
IRODOUER, Château du Quengo 27

JANZE, Château La Franceule 28
JOUE-LES-TOURS, Château de Beaulieu 64

LA BAULE, Castel Marie-Louise 36
LA CELLE-GUENAND, Château de la Celle-Guenand 65
LA FERTE-SAINT-AUBIN, Château les Muids 90
LA JAILLE-YVON, Château du Plessis 42
LACAVE, Château de la Treyne 131
LANDUJAN, Château de Léauville 29
LANGEAIS, Château de Chemilly 66
LARCAY, Château de Larcay 67
LARRA, Château de Larra 127
LE BREUIL-EN-BESSIN, Château de Goville 4
LE CHATELET-EN-BERRY, Château Estiveaux 47
LE MOLAY-LITTRY, Château du Molay 5
LE PIN, Château Saint-Roch 138
LE PORT-BOULET, Château des Réaux 68
LE PRE D'AUGE, Château du Pré d'Auge 6
LHERM, Château de Jottes 128
LOUBRESSAC, Château de Gamot 132
LUYNES, Domaine de Beauvois 69

MAILLEBOIS, Château de Maillebois 53
MARCAY, Château de Marcay 70
MARSEILLES-LES-AUBIGNY, Château d'Aubigny 48
MER, Château de Chantecaille 84
MERCUES, Château de Mercuès 134
MEULLES, Hostellerie du Château de Montfort 7
MONBAZILLAC, Château Rauly-Saulieut 104
MONCLAR D'AGENAIS, Château Le Seiglal 117
MONTBAZON, Château d'Artigny 71
MONTBAZON, Domaine de la Tortinière 72
MONTBRON, Château Saint-Catherine 93
MONTERRAUD, Château de Régagnac 105
MONTHOU-SUR-CHER, Château du Gué-Péan 85
MONTIGNAC, Château de Pur-Robert 106
MONTPINCHON, Château de la Salle 16

MONTPOUPON, Château de Montpoupon 73
MONTREUIL-SUR-LOIR, Château de Montreuil 43
MONTRICHARD, Château de la Menaudière 86
MONVIEL, Château de Monviel 118
MUIDS-SUR-LOIRE, Château de Colliers 84

NAZELLES, Château La Huberdière 74
NIEUIL, Château de Nieuil 94
NOGENT-LE-ROTROU, Château de l'Aulnay 54
NOTRE DANE DU GUIDO, Château du Val d'Arguenon 22

OIZON, Château de la Verrerie 49
ONZAIN, Domaine des Hauts-de-Loire 87
ONZAIN, Hôtel Château des Tertres 88

PERIGNY, Château de Périgny 99
PLEHEDEL, Château Hôtel de Coatguelen 23
PLEUGENEUC, Château de la Motte Beaumanoir 30
PLOMELIN, Château de Kerambleiz 25
POINTE DE PEN-LAN, Domaine du Château de Rochevilaine 34
POMMERIT-JAUDY, Château de Kermezen 24
PONT DE L'ARN, Château de Montlédier 137
PONT-L'ABBE, Château de Kernuz 26

QUINEVILLE, Château de Quinéville 17

RAZAC-SUR-L'ISLE, Château de Lalande 107
RAZINES, Château de Milly 75
REQUISTA, Château de Castelpers 124
RIGNAC, Château de Roumégouse 133
RILLY-SUR-LOIRE, Château de la Haute Borde 89
ROGNAC, Château de Rognac 108
ROSAY-SUR-LIEURE, Le Château de Rosay 12

SAINT-ANDRE-DU-BOIS, Château Malromé 113
SAINT-ANTOINE-DU-RUCHER, Château de la Mulonnière 76
SAINT-CHARTIER, Château de la Vallée Bleue 56
SAINT-EPIAN, Hostellerie du Château de Montgoger 77
SAINT-FOR-SUR-GIRONDE, Château des Salles 95
SAINT-HILAIRE-DE-COURT, Château de la Beuvrière 50
SAINT-NICOLAS DE LA BALERME, Château Saint-Philip 119
SAINT- OUEN-DES-VALLONS, Château de La Roche-Pichemer 45
SAINT-OUEN-LA-ROUERIE, Château des Blosses 31
SAINT-PATRICE, Hostellerie du Château de Rochecotte 78
SAINT-PIERRE-LA-FEUILLE, Château de Roussillon 135
SAINT- SYMPHORIEN-LE-CHATEAU, Château d'Esclimont 55
SALLES-CURAN, Hostellerie du Levézou 125
SAUTERNES, Château de Commarque 114
SAVIGNE-SUR-LATHAN, Château de Beaulieu 79
SERIGNY, Château de Saint-Bonnet 100

SOUSTONS, Château Bergeron 116
SURY-AUX-BOIS, Domaine de Chicamour 92

TERNAY, Château de Ternay 101
THAUMIERS, Château de Thaumiers 51
TOCQUEVILLE-EN-CAUX, Château de Rainfreville 21
TONNEINS, Castel Ferron 120
TOUR-EN-BESSIN, Château de Vaulaville 8
TOURVILLE, Château La Ricardière 13
TROO, Château de la Voûte 90

USSEAU, Château d'Olbreuse 96

VARETZ, Château de Castel Novel 102
VAUMICEL, Château de Vaumicel 9
VEYRIGNAC, Château de Veyrignac 109

Index of Châteaux with particular facilities

1. CHATEAU RESTAURANTS AWARDED A MICHELIN ROSETTE

★★
Hennebont, Château de Locguénolé 33

★
Anglet, Château de Brindos 121
Audrieu, Château d'Audrieu 1
La Baule, Castel Marie Louise 36
Luynes, Domaine de Beauvois 69
Marcay, Château de Marcay 70
Montbazon, Château d'Artigny 71
Montignac, Château de Puy-Robert 106
Montpinchon, Château de la Salle 16
Nieuil, Château de Nieuil 94
Onzain, Domaine des Hauts-de-Loire 87
Pléhédel, Château Hôtel de Coatguelen 23
Salles-Curan, Hostellerie du Levézou 125
Varetz, Château de Castel Novel 102

2. CHATEAUX WITHIN 15 KM OF AN AUTOROUTE

A10 64 67 77
A11 55
A13 6 11
A51 24
A62 110 118 119 120 138
A63 121 122 132
A71 90

3. CHATEAUX WITH PRIVATE SWIMMING POOL

1 5 7 23 25 29 32 33 34 44 55 64 69 70 71 72 77 80 93 94 99 102 104 106 109 111 112 115 116 117 118 121 126 129 131 132 134 136

4. CHATEAUX WITHIN 10 KM OF THE SEA

2 8 9 17 22 23 25 26 32 33 34 36 116 121 132

5. CHATEAUX WITHIN 20 KM OF A GOLF-COURSE

1 2 4 5 8 10 11 12 15 17 19 20 22 23 30 32 33 36 38 55 56 58 62 63 64 67 68 71 72 78 80 82 84 92 96 104 105 116 118 119 122 123 138

POSTSCRIPT

Lecture service
We are happy to give illustrated talks on the châteaux of France to organisations and groups.

Contributions required
Please send us your comments on the châteaux you have visited. The most interesting and informative will be included in the next edition.

Bon voyage.

SYD and ANNA HIGGINS
c/o Roger Lascelles,
Publisher,
47 York Road,
Brentford,
Middlesex,
TW8 0QP.